COPYRIGHT NOTICE

About Us

Right Mix Marketing Inc. is a leading search marketing consulting and training firm based in the San Francisco Bay Area.

- Our Web sites include:
  - www.RightMixMarketing.com
  - www.DirectionSEO.com

If you have consulting or training needs or need a speaker for an event or conference, please contact us.

How to use this manual

Welcome to the SEO Boot Camp. Here are a few pointers to getting the most out of this manual.

1. First, take a look at the Guide to Symbols on page 4 and the Table of Contents on pages 5 and 6. Get a feel for the flow of the book and the different chapters.

2. If you're at all unfamiliar with search engine terms, review the glossary in the appendices to learn some of the key terms before you start reading.

3. Start reading Chapter 1 on page 7. You'll get the most out of it if you take notes in a separate notepad as you go.
   - Questions that are triggered related to your site or business
   - Ideas that you get (e.g. areas of focus, competitors to check out, target customer types, keywords, tools to use and more)

4. It may make sense to make a copy of the templates and fill them out (at least a draft version) as you go through the chapters. The more you can integrate the lessons with your own business and site, the faster you'll actually get to the real work of improving your site's SEO.

5. Try out some of the tools or look at their Web sites as you go. Jot down the ones that you may want to look at in more detail.

6. Don't be afraid to go back and refine your work. SEO is an ongoing process and you can always refine things such as your target industries, customers, content or keywords

7. Don't get caught in analysis paralysis. The real value comes when you're actually out there testing techniques, creating content, marketing your site, building links or doing a PPC advertising test.

Okay, let's get started!

Guide to symbols used in this book

 Detailed information on a particular topic

 The **key point** of a particular topic or page

 Useful **tools** that can help you in a certain area

 Related **data** or **statistics**

 Common **mistakes** or **pitfalls**

 A **checklist** to help you keep track of key steps or options

---

SEO value:

Other value:

SEO: Page Titles are essential for ranking in search engines – just do it! **Other**: In addition to being a key item for ranking, your page titles also show up in the first line of a search result listing. Descriptive page titles greatly improve click-through rate by giving searchers a clear idea of the contents of the page.

Summary Assessment Box:
When you see box like this, it's designed to give you a quick assessment of the value of a certain technique or tool.

SEO Value*: Compared to other techniques, how important is this one in terms of improving your site's SEO?

Other Value*: Other than SEO Value, how can this help your online marketing efforts?

*These assessments are the judgment of Right Mix Marketing Inc. staff and are only provided as helpful guidelines.

Table of Contents

Chapter 1. Intro to Search Engines & Search Engine Optimization (SEO)

How do Search Engines help us find what we're looking for? What is SEO?

Contents

A. **Understanding Search Engines**

B. **Basics of Search Engine Optimization**

C. **Introduction to the Direction SEO Process**

What is a Search Engine?

A Search Engine is a tool that helps people find information on the Internet based on keywords that a searcher types into a search box.

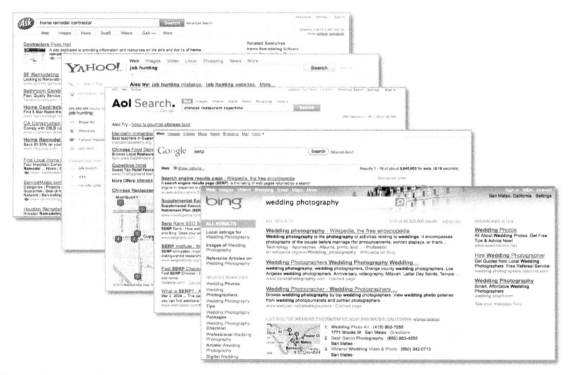

People usually access search engines by going to the main Web site of a search engine (e.g. www.Google.com, www.Yahoo.com, www.Bing.com).

In other cases, searches can be run directly from a Web browser (such as Internet Explorer, Firefox, Google Chrome, Safari or others). Often there is a search box at the top of the browser (or in Chrome's case the address bar can be used as a search bar for Google's search engine).

More and more frequently, people are accessing search engines on their mobile phones.

 In one month there are over 16B searches performed in the U.S.

*Source: comScore, www.comscore.com

8

What is a Search Engine Results Page (SERP)?

- A Search Engine Results Page (or "SERP") is a page of results from a search engine. It consists of:
  - Paid advertising (often in the form of pay-per-click text ads)
  - Organic (or "natural") search results which can include:
    - Links to Web pages that are relevant for the search
    - Links to videos, pictures or other documents as appropriate
    - Links to Social Media pages – such as a relevant user profile in LinkedIn, a Twitter post or a Facebook page
    - Pictures, information and pricing for products
    - Maps and reviews for local business listings
    - Stock quotes, news and charts

There are different types of Search Engine Results Pages (SERPs)

- Often, the search engines will choose the type of SERP to display depending on your query. Some types of of SERPs include:
  - News – the search results include content from news sites and will have recent articles on that topic
  - Current Events – the search results will have a heavy bias towards current content and news, gossip or Social Media types of sites
  - "How to" or Informational – this type of search will include long-standing "authoritative" articles and will often include videos which have "how to" information
  - Shopping – will include things such as products, reviews, ratings and prices
  - Pictures – will focus on pictures
  - Local – will include more local results and often a map and reviews

- In addition, the search engines are increasingly blending different types of results (news, pictures, video, Web sites, Social Media) into one SERP. This is called "universal search"

Search Trends to be aware of...

Universal Search

Up until early 2007, the results that you got when you ran a search on a search engine would be a collection of links taking you to various Web sites or documents (such as a PDF or Powerpoint document). In May of 2007 Google started to integrate other content into the main search results pages, calling this "Google Universal Search". This additional content included things such as pictures, videos, maps, recent news articles or stock quotes. More recently search results have been increasingly including links to Facebook pages, Twitter posts, LnikedIn profiles and other Social Media content relevant to your search. This trend to integrate a variety of types of content into the search results will only continue to build steam.

Real Time Search

A similar trend is happening when a search phrase is deemed to require current, information versus well-established authoritative Web pages. If the search engine sees that "Mel Gibson" happens to have a lot of recent searches and there are also news stories related to him, the search engines will put more importance on information that has been published recently for "Mel Gibson" searches. This same type of scenario could apply for a search such as "BP Gulf Coast" or "Meg Whitman CA Governor's race" where recent results are more important than a well-established corporate history of BP or a bio of Meg Whitman.

Local Search

A third major trend that is occurring in the name of helping you find what you want is Local Search. If you type "pizza" into a search engine, they're much more likely to give you the local pizza parlors and a map to them than they are to give you a history on pizza. Why? Because they are tuned to recognize searches that are most likely to be local in nature and the search engines now deliver results to help you find a good, local pizza place, a local store selling running shoes or a nearby doggy daycare service. This is especially true if you put a location term such as "bike store San Jose" in your search query.

Mobile Search

A fourth trend to be aware of us the Mobile Search. People are increasingly searching using their handheld mobile devices, especially smartphones like the Apple iPhone, Blackberries as well as Google's Android phones. People are using mobile versions of web browsers, specific search applications ("apps") such as Bing's and Google's iPhone apps, Yelp's application or maps applications.
Often mobile search will tie closely to local search as people are often searching for what's around them. Optimizing your local search presence can help you be found on mobile devices. In the future there will be more ways to specifically design your internet presence and online marketing (paid or organic) to target mobile phone users. In the meantime, focus on your basic SEO blocking and tackling to get more visibility via computer searchers. This should also draw in people who search via their mobile phones.

What do these trends mean for me?

What this means for you as a searcher? Better and more diverse search results from any given search.

What does this mean for your company? More opportunity to be found in different places and in different ways. Whether it be your Web site, your profile on LinkedIn, your videos in YouTube, your company tweets on Twitter or your company's Fan Page on Facebook.

Don't worry if you don't have most of this in place. The minimum to play in the search game is a Web site – we'll explain how this works and how the rest fit into your overall SEO strategy.

 There are many types of SERPs but the basic SEO tactics (covered in Chapter 6) remain the same

What are the components of a Google SERP?

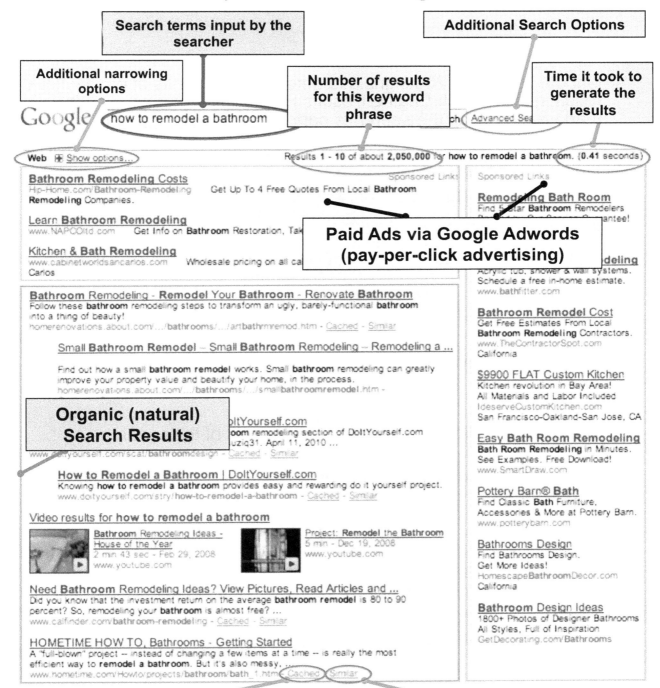

Search terms input by the searcher

Additional Search Options

Additional narrowing options

Number of results for this keyword phrase

Time it took to generate the results

Paid Ads via Google Adwords (pay-per-click advertising)

Organic (natural) Search Results

Shows the version of the page saved on Google's document server (may be different from the live version of the page)

Shows results similar to this listing

How do search engines decide which sites will "rank" highly in the organic (natural) search results?

- Google uses over 200 signals to determine the ranks of each result in the Search Engine Results Page. This determination is made real-time as the search is performed.

- It uses the signals to determine:
  - **Relevance** – based on keywords, content and the profile of inbound links, is the page relevant to the to the search query keywords?
  - **Authority** - based on the number and quality of inbound links and other factors is this page considered an authority in this topic area?
  - **Trust** – is the site trustworthy or is it linking with known spam sites?
  - **Visitor Experience** – does the site have quick page load time. lack of spam content and minimal broken links?

- They won't explicitly divulge all of the details of their search algorithms
  - Search engines don't want people to "game the system" and get high results via search spam

- How do you increases your Web site's rank in the search results?
  - **"Off-page" SEO** – getting high quality inbound links from other sites and communicating with the search engines
  - **"On-page" SEO** – keywords, content, page titles, optimizing video, pictures and more

What's the split of clicks between organic and paid listings in the SERPs?

Organic Search Results

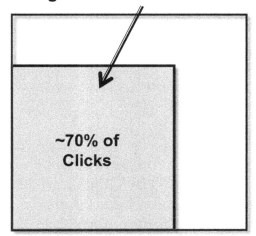

~70% of Clicks

Pay-Per-Click Ads

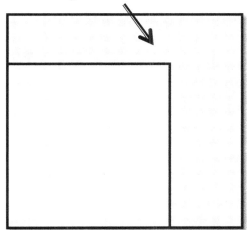

The organic search results in search engine results page.

- Get about 70% of the search clicks
- Have more trust from searchers because they're viewed as earned (not paid for)
- Can take time and significant SEO work to get on page one of the search results

The paid search results in search engine results page.

- Get about 30% of the search clicks
- May face some skepticism because they are known to be paid advertising
- Can be up and running with a pay-per-click advertising campaign within a day
- Are easily available for anyone to utilize but it takes budget and expertise to do it well
- Are a good place to do a test of your online marketing elements

 Organic results get about 70% of the clicks but ranking well can be hard to achieve for popular keyword phrases. Pay-per-click ads get about 30% of the clicks but you can be on page one within one day

Where do people click on a SERP?

The organic search results on a Search Engine Results Page get about 70% of the attention and clicks. In addition, most people will only click on a result on page 1. Often people will rerun a search with slightly different keywords if they don't see a suitable result on the first page. That's why getting in the first 10 results (page 1) is very important.

Within the organic results the 1st listing gets significantly more clicks than the 2nd and so on. In the analysis below (performed by Chitika, maker of an online advertising platform), the first position received double the clicks of the second position. There's quite a payoff in terms of traffic from getting ranked highly for popular keywords.

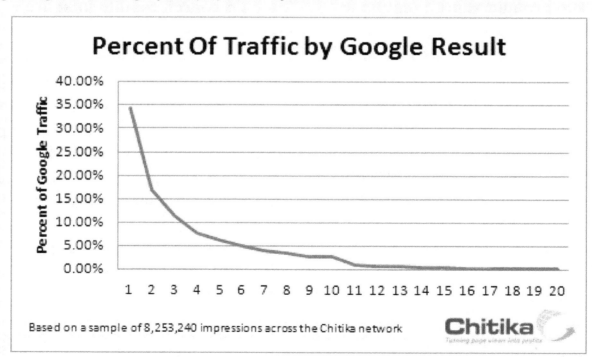

Source: Chitika, www.chitika.com

How a search works in Google

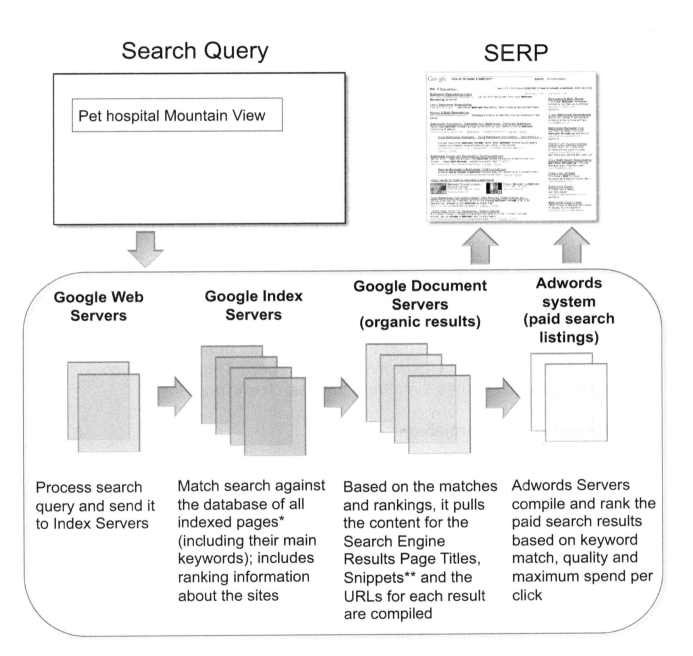

Search Query

Pet hospital Mountain View

SERP

Google Web Servers

Process search query and send it to Index Servers

Google Index Servers

Match search against the database of all indexed pages* (including their main keywords); includes ranking information about the sites

Google Document Servers (organic results)

Based on the matches and rankings, it pulls the content for the Search Engine Results Page Titles, Snippets** and the URLs for each result are compiled

Adwords system (paid search listings)

Adwords Servers compile and rank the paid search results based on keyword match, quality and maximum spend per click

*Google estimates that it has indexed over 1 trillion distinct URLs (unique addresses for Web pages)
**Snippets – The two lines in each Search Result under the Title that describe the page being linked to

Why is Google's search engine so much better than other search engines?

Hyperlinks (AKA "links") as votes

Google's big breakthrough in search was the development of using links to sites as "votes" for those pages. Prior to Google, the textual content of a Web page was the primary signal to the search engines about the page's focus. This system of judging pages based on content could easily be gamed leading to fairly low-quality search results.

PageRank to make some links count for more than others

Google's use of links as votes combined with the Google PageRank algorithm (which ranks the pages sending those links) allowed Google to determine in real-time which pages deserve to be higher in the search results for a given search query. This led to much better search results than the other search engines.

Minimal commercialism

Other factors that made Google a favorite in the early days included their stripped-down interface, devoid of in-your-face advertising. This famous white page featuring only a search bar and a couple of buttons really struck a chord with people tired of other sites and search engines displaying advertising or self-promoting content on every available square inch of Web real estate.

Speed of search

The stripped-down design (requiring less things to load on the page) as well as Google's investment in robust architecture has helped Google's search engine to be faster than its rivals.

Google is the 800 pound gorilla of search

For SEO you'll mainly be concerned with two Search Engines: Google and Bing. Yahoo has been using Bing's search results for the Yahoo search engine as of August 2010:

- **Google** – It typically has about 60-70% of the search market (depending on the month and who's measuring it). These results include YouTube searches but the bulk of the searches are through Google's main search engine. This should be your #1 focus for any SEO efforts.

- **Yahoo!** –Yahoo! had about 18% of the search market but has started using Bing's search results and advertising platform as of August 2010. You should focus any search efforts on Bing (as opposed to both Yahoo and Bing)

- **Bing** (Microsoft's new search engine) – it had about 12% of the search results (as of mid 2010). Microsoft is investing a lot of money and resources into improving the Bing search results as well as into marketing the engine so it will be improving and growing in usage.

Share of Searches

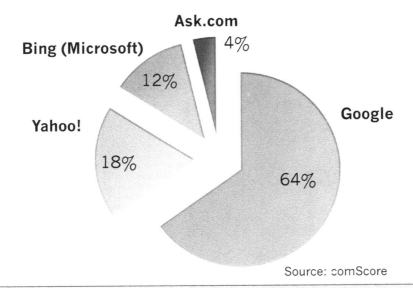

Source: comScore

 Google processes over 367 million searches per day in the U.S.!

Source: comScore

How does Google make so much money if its search engine is free?

Even though Google gives away its most popular product (search) for free, it's a very profitable company. In Q3 of 2010 it made profit of $1.84 billion on revenues of $5.09 billion. Google makes more than 90% of its revenues from search.

How? Mainly from the sponsored text ads at the top and the side of its free search results. It's the advertisers who use Google's Adwords system who foot the bill each time one of these ads is clicked on.

Google Inc.'s main revenue source – "sponsored links" via Adwords

What is Search Engine Optimization (SEO)?

- Search Engine Optimization (SEO) is the art and science of getting any given Web page to rank higher in the organic search results that come up when a searcher performs a search in a search engine

- It's the set of activities performed on a Web page ("on-page SEO") and outside of your Web site ("off-page SEO") that help influence your pages' positions in the search results for specific phrases

- SEO activities are designed to "signal" to search engines the following information:
  - Whether a page is **RELEVANT** for a particular topic or keyword phrase
  - Whether a page is considered an **AUTHORITY** for a particular topic or keyword phrase
  - Whether this site is **TRUSTWORTHY** by being associated with other trusted sites
  - Whether the site is **USER-FRIENDLY** for the searcher (to a lesser degree but this is becoming more important)

 SEO is the art and science of signaling your site's authority, trust, relevancy and user-friendliness to search engines

The Internet, Search and your timing for getting started with SEO

Over the last 15 years, the Internet has become firmly entrenched as a critical part of business. For major corporations, it's a key vehicle for building brand, providing information about products and services, making sales, delivering services and more. For small companies it's replaced the paper catalog, the yellow pages ad, and provides key information to prospective clientele.

Prior to any business meeting - whether a purchase, a sale, an interview or a partnership discussion, any business person worth his or her salt will consult the Web site of the other company to learn about the latest company news, to get a feel for the company culture, to learn about products and services, and possibly to see pictures, video or an article relating to the person they're about to meet! Pandora's box has been opened on the Internet and it won't be closing…

The Search Engines

Over the last 10 years, Search Engines have also become just as firmly entrenched in the way we live and the way we do business. What have you "Googled" lately? With the rise of Google and the company's faster, better search results, the bar was upped for search engines in general. People have come to appreciate the ease with which facts, pictures, Web pages, videos, presentations and more can be fetched from a computer or mobile phone thanks to ever-improving search technology which scours the Internet, catalogs its contents and serves up results based on your search query.

There are three major search engines (in the US) that vie for your attention. Google has about 65% share of the search market, Yahoo! has about 18% and Microsoft has about 12%. To fend off Google, Yahoo! and Bing have joined forces and are both using the Bing search results. In addition, Microsoft (Bing) has been heavily investing in its search capabilities. "Microhoo" (as the combination of Bing and Yahoo!'s search businesses is casually referred to) now has about 25-30% of the search market.

Well, am I too late to the game? The good news is that there's still a lot of opportunity to optimize your Web site for search engines to beat or gain ground on your competition. Here's why:

- **Change is constant:**
  - ○ Google and the other search engines are constantly changing their search "algorithms". This means that factors that cause a site to rank highly at one point in time may change and another site may rank higher due to a modification of the algorithm
  - ○ The search engines are now including more information in the searches (universal search). This means that instead of just links to Web pages or documents, search results now increasingly include pictures, videos, maps, product pricing, reviews, Twitter tweets, LinkedIn profiles and more. There are more ways for your company to be found online.

- **Many people have not optimized their sites yet:**
  - ○ Search Engine Optimization is still new enough that many people have not optimized their Web sites. In fact, many companies (big and small) don't even have great Web sites. There's still plenty of opportunity to leapfrog them with some basic SEO tactics.

- **You don't need to beat every site out there:**
  - ○ You just have to focus on the competition for your target keywords. The more defined your niche is, the less competitors you will be fighting against. For example, if you're optimizing your Web site for "Palo Alto Architects" you're limiting your competition significantly compared to optimizing for "California architects" or "Architects in the US"

It's a Marathon, not a Sprint...take your first steps. What all this means is that you're not too late to the game. There is still plenty of opportunity to improve your "findability" in the search engines and to beat your competitors by using basic, proven SEO fundamentals. It's a marathon (built over time) versus a sprint. Get started today with the initial steps.

What can SEO do for my company?

Level the playing field

What's interesting is that the Internet first, and now the search engines, have leveled the playing field for businesses of all sizes.

Why do I say that?

With the right strategy you can...

- Be easier to find in the search engines than your competitors
- Look bigger and more established than your competitors
- Have better information or tools than your competitors

...even if they are much bigger than your company

On the Internet even the smallest business can have a big and impressive presence.

This same small business can take orders internationally, can create a large online following and outwit the bigger guys.

 With effective SEO you can level the playing field and have a broader Web presence than even bigger competitors

---

The 10 Steps of the Direction SEO Process

At Direction SEO we follow the 10 step process described below. This process makes sure your SEO is tied to your company strategy, grounded in the right keywords and covers the most important activities that impact your search engine rankings.

Direction SEO Process

1. Tie your SEO Plans to Company Strategy

2. Understand your Customers and Competitors

3. Determine your Target Keywords

4. Get your Web site and Analytics Foundation in Place

5. Develop your SEO Balanced Scorecard

6. Do On-Page SEO Fundamentals

7. Do Off-Page SEO, mainly Inbound Link Building

8. Create Compelling Web site Content

9. Use Social Media to Drive Awareness and Links

10. Optional: Do a Paid Search Test for Keywords, Conversions, Positioning

 Follow a logical process to make your SEO efforts as effective and efficient as possible

Wrap up for the basics of SEO

- We covered these areas in this chapter:
    - **A. Understanding Search Engines**
    - **B. Basics of Search Engine Optimization**
    - **C. Introduction to the Direction SEO Process**

- You should now have a pretty good understanding of search engines, SEO and one process flow that you can follow in your SEO efforts.

- In this next chapter we'll get into Strategy, Customers and Competitors.

Chapter 2. Strategy, Customers, Competitors

Get your ducks in a row by lining up your
company strategy with your SEO strategy

<u>Contents</u>

A. **Aligning SEO with company strategy**

B. **Understanding your customers**

C. **Understanding your competitors**

Make sure your SEO efforts align with your company strategy

SEO, Web Design and Social Media activities take time and resources. It's important to waste as little time as possible on unfocused and strategically unaligned work. To use a car analogy, make sure you map out your route before you begin driving.

Before diving into the weeds of an SEO effort it's important to explicitly link your SEO, Web and Social Media strategies to your overall Company Strategy. This includes:

- What products/services you're trying to grow
- Which customer segments you're targeting
- How you're responding to competitors
- What you're doing in other areas of marketing

In addition, key groundwork should be done in the following areas:

- Understanding your customers and their typical buying cycle
- Knowing what your competitors are doing

 Focus your efforts by aligning your Company and SEO Strategies

Document your Company's Strategies and Priorities... and align your SEO efforts with them

For SEO to be effective it needs to support your overall strategy. The target keywords, content, conversion goals and link-building efforts all need to support the company's main goals and priorities.

Strategy Cascade

Company Strategy
Is the company opening a new location or going after a new market?
Is the company trying to staff up?
Is the company introducing a new product?
Is the company trying to severely cut costs?

Division Strategy
Similar to company strategy, what are the priorities for the division?

Product / Segment Strategy
What key products and services is the company focused on?
How do they need to be marketed differently?
What are the priority segments?
How do they research and purchase products or services?

Alignment

Sales and Marketing Strategies
How is the company marketing now, both online and offline?
What are the main sales channels?
Is there research, content or collateral that can be used for SEO?

Web and Social Media Strategy
How are your Web and Social Media strategies supporting the above?
What are your online conversion tactics?
How will you promote your site and content using Social Media (Twitter, Facebook, LinkedIn, etc.)?

SEO Strategy
Is there a current SEO Strategy, including: Target Keyword Phrases, Conversion Goals, Target Segments and Products, Link-building Strategy and Content Strategies

Why do you need to understand your customers?

In order to create an SEO strategy (including your conversion goals, keyword phrase targeting, content creation and link-building) you need to start with your customers:

- Who are they? Are they the same for all of your main products or do you serve several different segments?

- Which segments are most profitable? Which segments do you want to focus the most energy on?

- What are their wants, unspoken desires and needs?

- Who influences them? Where do they get their information?

- What is their search process? What keyword phrases do they use to find products/services like yours?

- Where do they research or buy products/services like yours?

The better you understand this up front the better your SEO efforts can specifically target your most valuable customers:

- Which products/services they buy

- How/where they buy

- How they search

- Which keyword phrases are most important

- Which content needs to be created to attract them

- Which conversions you want to target on your Web site

Don't be "me-focused" in your SEO or marketing. Focus on how customers find your type of business and what they would like to know

Develop Customer Personas and Understand Search/ Buying Behavior

One way to better understand your customers is to develop a persona for each customer group you want to target:

- **What's a persona?**
  - It's a composite of a typical customer
- **Can we have more than one persona?**
  - Yes, you can break down the types of people that buy from you (or even who influence the sale) and develop basic personas for the most important groups
  - You may have different personas for different products or services you sell
- **How do I do create the personas?**
  - Determine the types of customers that buy from you (brainstorm with your team, check your sales records, etc.)
  - Put them into groups - what are some common characteristics that your customers have that puts them into groupings?
  - Complete a persona template for each main group – this will help you with your keyword work in the next section
  - If possible, you can interview some of your customers or salespeople to get better information
  - The personas don't have to fit every customer exactly but give you a reasonable likeness of a typical customer from each of your main customer groups

 Personas are a way to make your typical customer types more real

Develop Personas for key customer types

Part 1: Lifestyle

Customer Persona #1 Title: (something descriptive of this customer group)	
Example Customer's Name (make up a name)	His/Her Current Occupation
Age, locale, marital status, kids, education level, etc.	Why do they want your products or services?
How/Where do they find your company or products/services?	What compels them to buy your products versus the competitors'?
What benefits do they get from using your products/services?	What objections might they have?

 Before you create an SEO plan, you should understand your customers – who they are, the benefits they receive from your products, how they buy and how they search

Develop Actionable Plans and Ideas for Each
Persona

Part 2: SEO Actionable Details

Customer Persona #1	
Main Products Purchased	Potential sites, blogs or Social Media sites they use or visit
Information they want from us (for use in content creation)	Create a landing page for them? What's on it? What conversions*?
How/Where do they search?	What keyword phrases would they use?
Key marketing messages for this group	Other notes or questions

*Conversions are actions that you want your potential customers to perform, getting them closer to becoming an actual customer. Conversions can include signing up for a newsletter, requesting a free consultation, making a purchase.

 You should use this persona information in your keyword selection, content creation and link-building efforts

Think about the typical buying cycle for your products

After you have your personas and understand the customers you want to focus on, you can then think about the typical buying cycle. You'll use this more in the next section on keywords but you may want to start thinking about:

- how your customers search
- what keywords they'll use at the different stages
- where you prefer to "hook them"
- what objections they'll have at each stage (and how to overcome them)

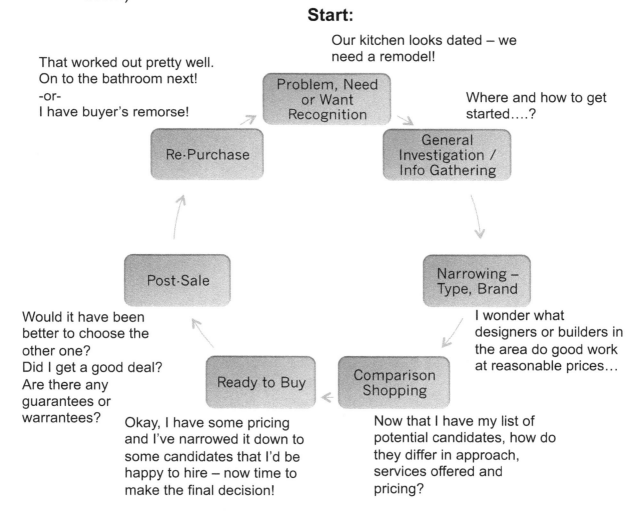

Start:

Our kitchen looks dated – we need a remodel!

That worked out pretty well.
On to the bathroom next!
-or-
I have buyer's remorse!

Problem, Need or Want Recognition

Where and how to get started….?

Re-Purchase

General Investigation / Info Gathering

Post-Sale

Narrowing – Type, Brand

Would it have been better to choose the other one?
Did I get a good deal?
Are there any guarantees or warrantees?

I wonder what designers or builders in the area do good work at reasonable prices…

Ready to Buy

Comparison Shopping

Okay, I have some pricing and I've narrowed it down to some candidates that I'd be happy to hire – now time to make the final decision!

Now that I have my list of potential candidates, how do they differ in approach, services offered and pricing?

Evaluating your competitors

Now that you have a pretty good feel for your customers, let's take a look at your competitors. You may have two types of competitors for each of your major products/services.

- **Type 1: Known "offline" competitors:**

    - These are the competitors that you already know about.

    - They're the companies that are selling what you sell locally (or nationally/internationally)

    - You bump into them or hear about them regularly

- **Type 2: Your "online" competitors:**

    - These are the competitors – either known or unknown that come up ranked highly when you type in some obvious keyword phrases for your business and customers

    - Make sure you narrow appropriately by product, geography or others keywords. If you're a local electronics store you want to see who's competing in your area. For example, use "home electronics San Francisco".

This is the first time you'll need to look at your competitors but not your last. This initial visit will help you get an idea of what your competitors are doing, how much catch-up work you have and it will also help you generate ideas for what you can be doing to stand apart from the crowd.

 You can learn a lot from your competitors. Take a look at who's coming up in the search results for your target keywords. You may be surprised.

Analyze of both types of competitors: Offline and Online

Known Offline Competitors:

Google their company name or visit their Web site if you know it. Then, evaluate their Web presence based on the following table.

"Online" competitors:

Pick a couple of obvious keyword phrases for each of your target products/services. Find the companies that are ranking highly for those phrases. Some may be the same as the known offline competitors, others may be new to you. Then, evaluate their Web presence using the following table.

Competitor Evaluation Template				
Competitor Name and URL	**Keyword phrases ranking highly for**	**Target Keyword phrases**	**Good content on site and Blog**	**Conversions**
Competitor 1	Which keywords, if any, are they ranking well for?	Which phrases show up in their page titles and content?	What content do you think is attractive to their (and your) target customers? Are they blogging effectively?	What conversions are they trying to get?
Social Media Usage	**Keyword ideas**	**Content/Blog ideas**	**Conversion ideas**	**Social Media ideas**
What are they doing with Social Media?	Document keyword phrases you may want to use	Document content ideas that you get. Any ideas for your blog?	What conversion ideas does this give you?	What Social Media approaches may work for you company?

Focusing your efforts on the right keyword
phrases for your market

Contents

A. **Keywords and how they fit in the buying cycle**

B. **Why keyword choice matters**

C. **The concept of long tail and keywords**

D. **Keyword list development process**

Why are keywords important for SEO?

The search engines use algorithms to determine how billions of Web pages should rank for any given search. This is all done in an automated fashion and usually takes less than a second.

Importance of keywords:

- Play a significant role in determining which searches your Web page will show up for. Those Web pages that contain keywords that match a search term, that are trustworthy and have authority (in the eyes of search engines) are going to rank higher than sites that don't.

- Keywords are also important when used in "anchor text" of links connecting one Web page to another. The text used to describe a link to a page is another important signal to telling a search engine what the destination page is about.

- Knowing your target keywords allows you to track your SEO progress – without knowing what you're trying to rank for, you're lacking a way to track this.

- Keywords allow you to focus your efforts and to prioritize which areas you'll focus the most energy on.

- Keyword research allows you to find out how often people use keywords in searches and helps you use the best keywords for the topic you'd like to rank for.

If you don't clearly communicate what your Web pages are about (by using the best keyword phrases for your business) then your site will not come up in the search results you want to be coming up for.

This chapter further explores keyword phrases and why choosing the right phrases is very important for your company.

 You communicate to search engines through the content and keywords on your Web pages and via the links (and the words used in those links) that your site attracts from other sites

How many words do people use in their search queries?

Most searches are multiple word keyword phrases. According to the Experian Hitwise data shown below, 77% of searches are 2 or more words. You want to target 2-3 word phrases that are very relevant for your company and its products/services but that also have enough search volume.

Percentage of U.S. clicks by number of keywords			
Subject	April 2010	May 2010	Month-over-month percentage change
One word	22.77%	22.46%	-1%
Two words	23.06%	23.34%	1%
Three words	20.31%	20.51%	1%
Four words	14.23%	14.24%	0%
Five words	8.55%	8.53%	0%
Six words	4.71%	4.66%	-1%
Seven words	2.60%	2.56%	-2%
Eight or more words	3.78%	3.70%	-2%

Note: Data is based on four-week rolling periods (ending May 1, 2010, and May 29, 2010) from the Hitwise sample of 10 million U.S. Internet users.

Source: Experian Hitwise

 Almost 20% of searches are 5 or more words long

Where you fit in the buying cycle

When thinking about keywords, it helps to put them in the context of the buying cycle. That way you can select keywords that are at the right stages of the cycle for your company.

Discounters
Some companies prefer to have other companies provide all of the education and then these discounters will try to get customers as they comparison shop for prices using keyword phrases such as "Nike cross trainers cheap" or "discount shoes".

Lead Nurturers
Other companies would rather get people early in the research stage and then nurture this person through the buying cycle with education and robust content until they're finally ready to purchase. These types of companies do well by getting the people to subscribe to their email newsletters, download their white papers, watch videos and more. The potential customers grow familiar with the company and grow to trust their expertise.

...and Every Type of Company In-Between
It helps to know where your company wants to fit in the buying cycle. Are you willing to educate and "nurture" your leads? Or are you fairly transactional – hoping to find ready and willing buyers and to convince them with your prices (or potentially unique products, product quality or purchasing terms)? Are you willing to move up in the cycle and to increase your engagement and education of potential buyers?

Lead Nurturers look for people early in the research stage
• These types of companies want to get customers on their email list, Twitter feed or Facebook Page and they'll educate them until they're ready to buy

Discounters look for people at this stage
• They want the customers when they're ready to buy and they'll try to get you with low prices

For higher value sales, it typically requires more "touches" with the customer – so more of a lead nurturing approach

Search terms in the buying cycle

Problem, Need or Want Recognition

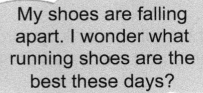

My shoes are falling apart. I wonder what running shoes are the best these days?

Low readiness to buy → **High readiness to buy**

General Investigation / Info Gathering

"How to pick a running shoe"
"Best running shoes"
"Top-selling running shoes"
"Best Nike running shoes for men"

Narrowing by Type, Brand

"Nike reviews"
"Asics reviews"
"Running shoe ratings"

Comparison Shopping

"Nike comparison shopping"
"Nike shoe prices"

Ready to Buy

"San Jose shoe store coupons"
"buy Nike running shoes"
"Price Nike Air Max running shoes"
"Discount shoe stores"
"Cheap Nike shoes online"

Post-Sale

Re-Purchase

Did I get the best deal?
They're not as comfortable as I hoped!
What's the return policy?

Why keyword choice matters…

You may think all similar keyword phrases are basically interchangeable and just as valuable for your SEO efforts. But they're not…

Let's look at an example:

Let's say you're the producer of Event and Meeting Software (which streamlines the planning and management activities) and you're launching a new Web site along with an online marketing campaign. Which of the following keyword phrases would you focus the most energy on?

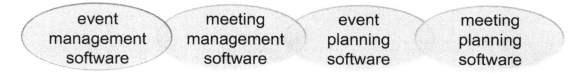

event management software　meeting management software　event planning software　meeting planning software

- What things would you consider in your choice?
- Where would you look to find more information?

Some companies make up their own words for their products or services to be unique and to stand out in the marketplace. This is a big mistake for SEO! Don't call your cars "people transportation devices". No one will find you online if you don't use words that they use in their search queries.

Now we layer on the number of searches per month (from the Google Keyword tool)

Searches per Month*

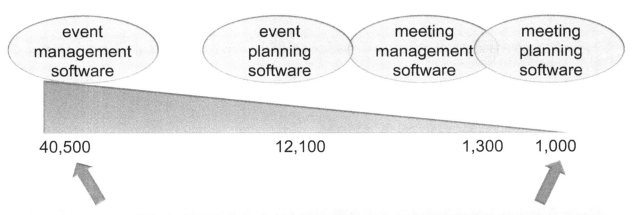

Event management software has **40 times** the number of searches/month as **meeting planning software!**

Of course there are other factors to consider before we focus all of our efforts on "event management software":
- Relevance with your customer intent
- The primary market for your specific product
- Your customer's purchase behavior
- Conversion rate for different keywords
- Amount and strength of competitors for different keywords

 All Keyword Phrases are not created equal. Make sure your chosen phrases match your target customer type, are at the right part of the purchase cycle and have significant enough volume

*Data Source: Google Adwords Keyword Tool

Getting Search Traffic Estimates
(using Google Keyword Tool)

Go to www.Google.com/Adwords/KeywordTool/external and follow these steps:

1) Put in representative keywords for your business and run the search.

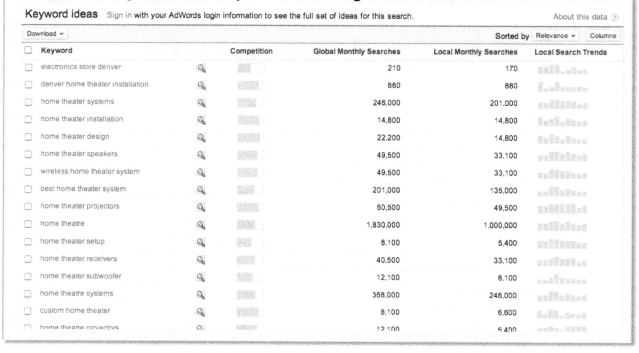

2) The keywords will come out sorted by relevance. You can also sort by volume to get a list of keywords from high traffic to low.

Keyword		Competition	Global Monthly Searches	Local Monthly Searches	Local Search Trends
electronics store denver			210	170	
denver home theater installation			880	880	
home theater systems			246,000	201,000	
home theater installation			14,800	14,800	
home theater design			22,200	14,800	
home theater speakers			49,500	33,100	
wireless home theater system			49,500	33,100	
best home theater system			201,000	135,000	
home theater projectors			60,500	49,500	
home theatre			1,830,000	1,000,000	
home theater setup			8,100	5,400	
home theater receivers			40,500	33,100	
home theater subwoofer			12,100	8,100	
home theatre systems			368,000	246,000	
custom home theater			8,100	6,600	
home theatre projectors			12,100	5,400	

Keyword ideas Sign in with your AdWords login information to see the full set of ideas for this search. About this data ⑦

Download ▾ Sorted by Relevance ▾ Columns

3) In the same search you can also find out what types of things people are interested in learning about – great topics for your blog posts!

how to install home theater system		2,900	2,400	
installing home theater systems		1,600	1,300	
installing a home theater system		1,600	1,300	
best home theater speakers		49,500	33,100	
best home theater speaker		49,500	40,500	
how to set up home theater system		12,100	9,900	
home theater systems design		22,200	18,100	
home theater system design		22,200	18,100	
how to design a home theater system		22,200	18,100	
home theater systems setup		8,100	5,400	
home theater speaker installation		49,500	40,500	
new home theater systems		246,000	201,000	
home theaters systems		246,000	201,000	
in home theater system		201,000	165,000	
quality home theater systems		720	390	
small home theater systems		246,000	201,000	
home theater system set up		12,100	9,900	

Go to page: 1   Show rows: 50   ◄ ◄ 1 - 50 of 800 ► ►|

4) You can export all of the words or selected words (and all of their data) into a Microsoft Excel or other spreadsheet.

The concept of "The Long Tail"

The Long Tail refers to the concept that in a category of items, there are going to be a small number of items that are popular and many others that are not as popular. The large volume of less popular items forms a long tail when put out on a graph as you see below for the music industry.

The Music Business Then and Now:

In the music business in the "old days" you had hit albums (or CD) and you had a lot of other records (or CDs) that did not sell well. So, for example, you might have had a Madonna album that was a top-seller, selling hundreds of thousands of CDs. In the same year, you might have had a CD by Thelonious Monster (an obscure Los Angeles band) that sold a few hundred copies. All of the low volume items make up the "tail" of the graph below.

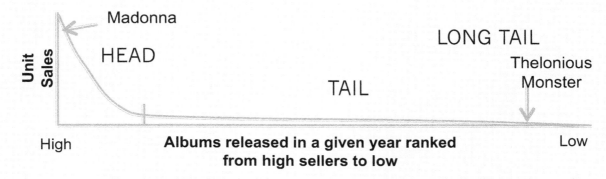

In the old days where a CD had to be kept in stock in a record store, it was not profitable to keep a lot of the less popular or niche bands' albums in stock. That's why most record stores would focus on the big-sellers and would try to get rid of anything that didn't sell in some sort of volume.

The Long Tail and the Internet

In 2004, Chris Anderson, the editor of Wired Magazine described in the magazine (and then a book) this concept as it applies to the Internet. In the Internet where storage costs approach zero for digital products and shelf space (e.g. your Internet site) is only limited by the effort you put into it, businesses can actually be profitable serving the long tail. All of the purchases of the obscure and niche products add up to as much, if not more sales than the hits.

So, Apple iTunes, for example, can stock much more niche and obscure music at very low incremental cost – many more than any brick-and-mortar CD store can afford to stock.

What does this mean for SEO?

You can apply the long tail logic to search as well. There are many searches for major generic keywords. So the keywords at the "Head" (high volume) would be something like "Electronics" or "Electronics Store". These type of keyword phrases will have hundreds of thousands of searches per day.

If you focus on the popular keyword phrase "electronics store" and really optimize your site and link-building efforts, you'll still probably never be able to get on the first page of Google's SERP. Why not? Because the popular keywords with high volume also tend to have the highest competition. All the companies in similar businesses or that are marketing to people interested in electronics will be fighting for the "electronics store" keyword phrase.

Your Strategy

In order to rank for relevant keywords, you want to do a couple of things:

1)   Make your main target keywords more specific to your business so you can face less competition and also get more relevant and qualified traffic.

- For example (use keyword tools to pick out "mid tail" keywords that have enough volume). Some ideas could be:
    - Colorado Springs electronics store
    - Colorado Springs audio video
    - Home audio installation
    - Denon tuner Colorado
    - Home theater installer Colorado Springs

2)   Use your blog to use various niche, specialized and location-specific keywords in meaningful articles. Write blog posts over time that add to the variety of mid-tail and long-tail keyword phrases contained within your site.

- For example (write how-to posts, customer success stories, product reviews, etc.)
    - Denon XYZ receiver top 5 features explained– video (and written) how to use 5 unique features
    - Colorado Springs High Fi Electronics Store's top 20 audio and video components ranking
    - Case Study – Colorado Springs resident installs professional-grade home theater using mid-price components. How to with photos!

Casting multiple lures

One way to think about it is as follows. Each unique and relevant keyword phrase that you use on your Web site (especially if used in page titles, headers and within the content) is like an additional lure you're casting into the search "ocean". The more focused those keyword phrases are, the more likely your site is to come up when that phrase, or a very similar one, is typed into the search engines.

Obviously the volume of these searches is lower for these niche phrases so the more varied (but relevant) phrases you're able to put into your Web site content, the better. Also, your blog is a perfect place to write short, targeted posts (or to host videos, photos or white papers with proper description) so the search engines can find your niche keyword phrases.

To read more about The Long Tail:
http://longtail.typepad.com/the_long_tail/2005/09/long_tail_101.html

Head vs. Tail Keywords

Head
- Generic keywords
- Common and popular topics
- Shorter keyword phrases

Shoot for the "mid-tail" for your SEO:
- 2-3 word phrases
- Define your niche as much as possible
- Define your products/services to the next level of granularity

Your blog can help you cover "mid-tail" words and some of the "long tail"
- Articles on niche topics
- Variety of keywords

Long Tail:
- More obscure topics
- Longer keyword phrases
- Misspellings

Cost and Competition (vertical axis)

High   **Frequency of searches**   Low

Example of Head vs. Tail Keywords

Software – 226 K/mo

Event Software – 70K/mo

Event Management Software – 41K/mo

Corporate Event Management Software – 8.1K/mo

Online Event Registration Software – 2.4K/mo

Event Management Registration Software – 2.4K/mo

Conference Planning Software – 1.6K/mo

Meeting Registration Software– 590/mo

Online Event Registration Systems– 28/mo

 Searchers increasingly type in longer queries to try to answer specific questions. If you blog on a variety of topics related to your industry and include "narrowing keywords" such as your city, product type or problem solved it can help your pages rank higher for the long tail searches

Bigger is not always better - use local and niche-specific keywords to cut competition

Comparison of Top Search Result for Different Keyword Phrases

Number of Pages Google has in index for the keyword:	Top Search Result Company:	Top Result Company Type:
284,000,000 for **electronics**	Sony Electronics (National)	National brand
41,100,000 for **car electronics**	Crutchfield.com	National brand
1,530,000 for **japanese car electronics**	Yano Research	Niche company – long tail keyword phrase happened to match well with a white paper they wrote
663,000 for **car electronics bay area**	Audio Symphony (in San Francisco)	Regional player with good SEO
72,500 for **car electronics san mateo**	Soundwave Mobile Electronics (in San Carlos)	Local company, neighboring city
14,700 for **car electronics millbrae**	Audio Symphony (in San Francisco)	Regional player with good SEO. There is likely no local company with good SEO optimized for Millbrae (a missed opportunity for someone)

 Use Niche and Local keywords to be a bigger fish in a smaller pond.

Keyword List Development Steps

1) Determine which Section of your Web site and which Products/Services you'll focus on first

- For your homepage the keyword phrases can be more generic with more specific keywords for product/service sections
- Focus on one major section at a time

2) List out the Obvious Keywords for that product, product type, brand

- Product, product type, industry, brands, problems solved
- Local keywords – cities, counties served or targeted

3) Brainstorm additional potential keyword phrases

- Think like a customer – what would you type to find your products, services or company?

4) Interview customers, sales or other stakeholders

- How do they search?
- What keywords do they use?

5) Bring in other external data for more ideas; purge irrelevant keywords from your master list

- What keywords are the competitors using on their pages?
- What do you see when you do some searches using the keywords you've already collected?
- Your Web site analytics – what are people using now to find your site?
- Blogs, forums, YouTube, etc.

6) Make "Keyword Clusters"- cluster similar keywords into logical groupings

- Make groups of related keywords, including high traffic "Main Keyword Phrases" and "Supporting Keyword Phrases"

7) Use keyword tools to get quantitative data and related keywords

- Use Google Keyword Tool or other keyword tools to get traffic estimates

8) Finalize clusters

- Based on the traffic and also keyword relevance, adjust your clusters
- Designate Main Keyword Phrases and Supporting Keyword Phrases

9) Document negative keywords, common misspellings, slang and potential niche keywords for future use

- Negative keywords are words you found that are very irrelevant for your company
- Relevant, niche keywords can be good for blog posts, whitepapers or videos

10) Utilize your Keyword Clusters in your SEO, advertising and Social Media activities

- Keeping related keywords together in sections of your Web site helps emphasize what that page is focused on

 Further details on these steps follow in the next pages

3) Brainstorm additional potential keyword phrases

A. Find a place and time to brainstorm without interruption; schedule an hour per major Web site section

B. Brainstorm keywords and keyword phrases that people may use in search engines to find your company, products or solutions

- Collect ideas on large sticky notes that you can read from far away and can move around
- Everyone spends 10 minutes writing their ideas from one keyword up to 3 or 4 word phrases on large sticky notes
- After 10 minutes, each person reviews their ideas out loud and starts to post them in logical clusters
- As new ideas come to people, feel free to call them out, write them and add them to the clusters
- In brainstorming, allow all ideas (no matter how strange) and don't criticize or argue against ideas

C. Once everyone has gone through their lists, adjust the groupings as appropriate

D. Use the brainstorming results as input for the next step in the process

You may think about your products using a certain set of keywords (including internal jargon). Don't think your customers think the same as you! They probably use very different keywords to do their research – you may be surprised! Ask them…

When brainstorming, think along these lines:

- Problems people are trying to solve – e.g. "fix leaky pipes" or "broken toilet" for plumber

- Product categories – "American made trucks"

- Brands – "buy HP multimedia computer"

- Associated products – "buy computer" (for company selling mice and keyboards)

- What people want – "remodel my kitchen" for a contractor

- Events – "wedding present", "bachelorette party"

- Seasonal - "Valentine's Day", "Christmas", "Winter"

- Key modifiers – "best", "cheapest", "fast"

- Location – e.g. "California", "Los Angeles", "Bay Area"

- Abbreviations – "PC" (computer), "SEO", "DIY" (do-it-yourself)

- Synonyms – "notebook", "laptop"

- Singular vs. Plural – "photographer", "photographers"

 Local will always have less competition. If you're a locally-oriented business, you need to optimize your site for your main local keywords

- A **Keyword Cluster** is a group of relevant phrases (5-15 phrases) that usually share at least two of the same keywords and are thematically similar. You would use these clusters to develop focused Web pages, articles or advertising campaigns focused on the cluster.

- **Main Keyword Phrase**: Usually each cluster would have one main keyword phrase. This phrase is highly relevant to your company and generally will be the highest trafficked phrase amongst the phrases in the cluster.

  - For example, a photographer could have "Anaheim wedding photographer" as the Main Keyword Phrase for one of his/her clusters

- **Supporting Keyword Phrases**: These are related to the Main Keyword Phrase, are still highly relevant but may be slightly more specialized or have slightly less search traffic (use a keyword research tool for traffic estimates)

  - For our wedding photographer, supporting keyword phrases (for "Anaheim wedding photographer") could include:

    - Anaheim wedding photography

    - Anaheim wedding photographers

    - Etc…

Main Phrase   Supporting Phrases

Cluster 2

Orange County Wedding Photographer

Orange County wedding photography
Orange County wedding photographers
Orange County marriage photographer
Top Orange County wedding photographer
Best Orange County wedding photographer
Orange County wedding pictures

Cluster 1

Anaheim Wedding Photographer

Anaheim wedding photography
Anaheim wedding photographers
Anaheim marriage photographer
Top Anaheim wedding photographer
Best Anaheim wedding photographer
Anaheim wedding pictures
Professional wedding photographer

Cluster 3

Anaheim Baby Photographer

Orange County baby photographer
Professional baby photographer
Best baby photographers
Etc….

Keyword clusters are groupings of related keywords – typically with one main phrase and other, related phrases

Turning keyword tool data into Keyword Clusters

Keyword	Competition	Monthly Searches
event software	1	74000
event management software	1	40500
event planning software	1	12100
event registration software	1	12100
online event registration	1	9900
online registration software	1	9900
corporate management software	0.93	8100
online event management	1	5400
online event planning	1	4400
online event software	0.87	4400
event management training	1	4400
event production companies	1	3600
conference registration online	0.87	2900
conference management software	1	2400
event registration management software	1	2400
event management registration software	0.8	2400
online event registration software	1	2400
event registration system	1	1900
event marketing software	0.87	1900
conference registration software	1	1600
event scheduling software	1	1600
conference scheduling software	1	1600
meeting management software	1	1300
event management program	1	1300
event planning program	1	1300
event registration service	1	1300
event planning tools	1	1000
meeting planning software	1	1000
free event planning software	0.8	1000
free event management software	0.73	1000
web registration software	0.93	1000
events management software	1	880
online event management software	0.93	880
conference planning software	1	720
event management tool	0.93	720
event manager software	0.93	720
event management database	1	720
corporate planning software	0.93	720
meeting registration software	1	590
meeting planner software	1	590
online event registration system	1	590
web based event management	0.8	590
web based event registration	0.93	590
event planning tool	0.93	480
online event registration service	1	480
conference registration system	0.93	480
trade show management software	0.8	390
web based registration software	0.8	390
open source event management software	0.53	390
seminar registration software	0.93	390
software for event management	0.67	320
free event registration software	0.67	320
online conference registration software	0.93	320
online event registration services	0.93	320
corporate event planning software	1	210
event managment software	0.8	210
attendee management software	0.8	210
event organizer software	0.53	210
professional event planning software	0.6	210
event planning software microsoft	-	210
security event management software	0.73	210
meeting room management software	0.8	210
web based event management software	0.73	170
event management system software	0.67	170
event registration tools	0.93	170
meeting management tool	0.53	170
church event software	0.8	170
on line registration software	0.8	170
conference registration systems	0.87	170
events planning software	0.8	140
meetings management software	0.6	140
tradeshow management software	0.67	140
software for event registration	0.73	140
event registration solution	0.93	140
convention registration software	0.93	140
online event scheduling	0.6	110
conference planning tools	0.6	91
meeting management tools	0.6	91
event planning software with	0.2	91
web based event planning software	0.27	73
best event management software	0.53	73
events registration software	0.87	73
restaurant event planning software	0.67	73
best event planning software	0.47	58
event management software review	0.47	58
convention planning software	0.53	58
meeting planner tools	0.73	58
event planning software reviews	0.33	46
event management software reviews	0.4	46
event management software comparison	0.4	46
event registration program	0.8	46
online event registration systems	0.87	28

Source: Google Keyword Tool

Possible Keyword Clusters

Event Management Software 74K/mo
- online **event management** 8.1K/mo
- **event management** registration software 2.4K/mo
- **event management** program 1.3K/mo
- free **event management** software 1.0K/mo

Event Planning Software
- online event planning
- event planning program
- event planning tools
- free event planning software

Event Registration Software
- Etc...

Try to group your Keyword Clusters with two words in common per phrase if possible

10) Utilize your Keyword Clusters in your SEO, advertising and Social Media activities

Where do you I use my keyword clusters?

- ## On your Web site
    - Structure your Web site based on how people search and using target keyword clusters
    - Build out pages focused on relevant clusters including the main keyword phrase and supporting keyword phrases
- ## On your blog
    - Use target keyword phrases in blog posts, categories and tags
    - Allow yourself to use alternate phrasing and to drill deeper into more niche topics (and phrases) to get long tail searches
- ## In your pay-per-click campaigns
    - Structure Ad Groups based on your clusters
- ## In your other marketing efforts, including Social Media
    - Use the same phrases throughout your marketing efforts
- ## In your SEO scorecard or measurement system
    - Track your rankings in the search engines for you target keywords

Having a well-defined niche or customer group is one of your best weapons in SEO. Exploit it!

Align and reinforce keyword usage in all aspects of your marketing

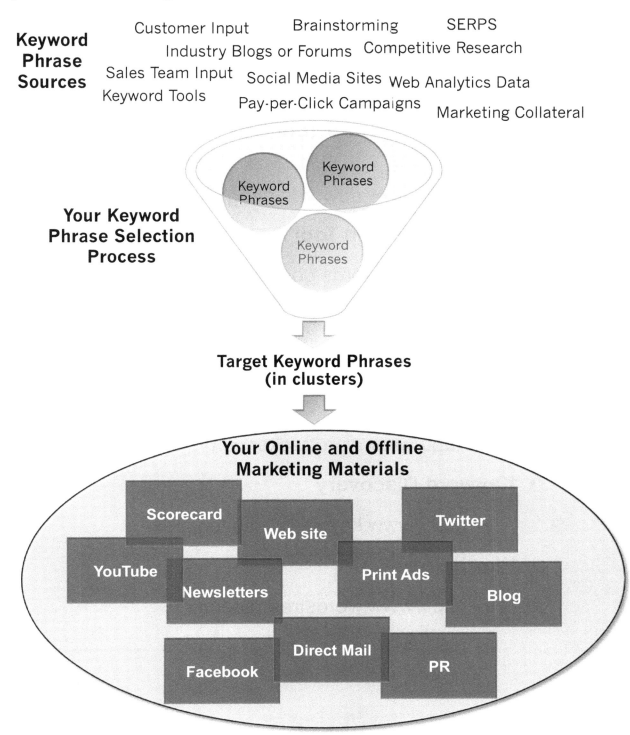

Keyword Phrase Sources

Customer Input   Brainstorming   SERPS

Industry Blogs or Forums   Competitive Research

Sales Team Input   Social Media Sites   Web Analytics Data

Keyword Tools   Pay-per-Click Campaigns

Marketing Collateral

Your Keyword Phrase Selection Process

Keyword Phrases

Keyword Phrases

Keyword Phrases

Target Keyword Phrases (in clusters)

Your Online and Offline Marketing Materials

Scorecard

Web site

Twitter

YouTube

Newsletters

Print Ads

Blog

Facebook

Direct Mail

PR

Keyword Research Tools

- **Google Keyword Tools (Free)**

  - **Adwords Keyword Tool** (free with Adwords account)

    - http://www.adwords.google.com/

  - **Google Keyword Tool External**

    - https://adwords.google.com/select/KeywordToolExternal

- **Other Keyword Tools (paid)**

  - **WordTracker**

    - http://www.wordtracker.com/

  - **Keyword Discovery**

    - http://www.keyworddiscovery.com/

  - **Wordstream**

    - http://www.wordstream.com/

Keywords Wrap up

In this chapter we covered the following topics:

A. **Keywords and how they fit in the buying cycle**

B. **Why keyword choice matters**

C. **The concept of long tail and keywords**

D. **Keyword list development process**

You should now be able to develop a target keyword list with keyword clusters that consist of Main Keywords and Supporting Keywords. Don't worry, you can refine your list over time – no list starts out perfect. The important thing is to start getting your list "on paper". This will help you focus your SEO work.

In the next chapter we'll cover your Web site and the importance of integrating analytics into it.

Chapter 4. Web site and Analytics

Is your Web site built on a solid foundation? Do you know how many people visit your site and where they spend their time?

Contents

In the big picture, how should your Web site play into your marketing strategy?

Your Web site is a key part of your online marketing strategy

Web site Visitors

Keep them engaged

- Videos
- How-to's
- Blog posts
- Selection guides
- Training
- Entertainment

Make sales

- Products
- Services
- Memberships
- Consultations
- Trial offers

Provide opportunities to extend relationship

- Newsletter sign-ups
- RSS feed sign-ups
- Twitter follower
- Facebook fan

 Are you engaging your audience? Providing ways to extend the relationship beyond this one visit? Providing opportunities to make conversions and sales?

Which type of Web site do you have?
Four competing priorities of Web design

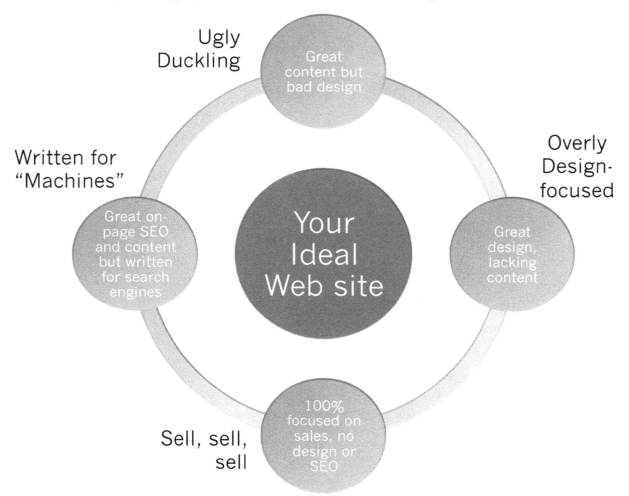

Ugly
Duckling

Great
content but
bad design

Overly
Design-
focused

Written for
"Machines"

Great on-
page SEO
and content
but written
for search
engines

Your
Ideal
Web site

Great
design,
lacking
content

Sell, sell,
sell

100%
focused on
sales, no
design or
SEO

- Your Web site should be attractive and clean but design is not everything

- Focus on a generous amount of quality content; make sure it's appealing both to people <u>and</u> search engines

- Don't be only focused on the sale but make sure you (and your visitors) are clear on the conversions you're trying to achieve

 You should strive to have great content, an attractive site and SEO in place, but with a clear focus on conversions

Use the best Web site technology for your business

- Your Web site is a critical part of your SEO strategy. Two key aspects of SEO which are directly impacted by your Web site include:

  1. **On-Page SEO Fundamentals:** The ability to edit URLs, title tags, meta tags, alt tags and links to be more SEO-optimized (see chapter 6)

  2. **Keyword-rich Content:** The ability to easily add keyword-rich content focused on your target keyword phrases (see chapter 9)

- With many Web sites, the technology makes it difficult for all but the most technical person to implement #1 (On-Page SEO Fundamentals). In addition, adding #2 (Keyword-rich Content) is time-consuming because it requires the creation of new pages and also manual updates to the navigation on the other pages so people can access the new content.

- Over the last few years there have been developments that allow new Web sites to be created and updated much more quickly than before. These include the development of:

  - **Content Management Systems (CMS)** – these Web publishing platforms allow for easy Web site or blog creation and management. You can use these CMS platforms on your own Web host ("self-hosted", i.e. you're responsible for finding your own hosting and paying for it) or some of them provide for a hosted solution (hosted by the CMS company).

    - Self-hosted examples: Wordrpess.org platform, Joomla, Drupal

    - Hosted examples: Wordpress.com platform, Blogger.com, CushyCMS, PageLime

  - **Shopping Cart platforms** – specialized platforms that allow you to create a Web store and shopping cart for sales of multiple products (both hosted and self-hosted versions are available)

    - Examples: Yahoo Shopping, Shopsite, Shopify

- Your Web site technology choice will impact your customer experience, your ability to meet your business goals and your SEO capabilities for a significant amount of time. Choose the technology you use wisely. We'll review some of the options and selection criteria over the next few pages.

For good SEO and ease of adding content, a Content Management System (CMS) is recommended for most new Web sites

Options	Hosting	Ability to do On-page SEO	Ease of adding content	Recommended?	Why or why not recommended?
HTML-based Site	Self-hosted	**Can be high**	**Low**	**No**	• On-page SEO can be accomplished but it is time-consuming and requires technical skill • Adding content also takes more time and effort than a CMS so it usually is not added as frequently as it should be
Flash-based Site	Self-hosted	**Low**	**Low**	**No**	Flash sites are usually visually very appealing. Drawbacks are: • Search engines have a hard time reading the text on flash sites • Many aspects of On-page SEO can't be done in Flash • Non-technical people can't easily add new content to a flash-based site
Self-hosted CMS (or blog platform)	Self-hosted	**Medium to High**	**High**	**Yes**	• On-page SEO can often be accomplished fairly easily with a CMS • Adding new content is very easy even for non-techies • Usually cheaper to set up due to the availability of pre-designed skins or templates and re-use of the CMS system
Hosted CMS (or blog platform)	Hosted by the CMS or blog platform company	**Low**	**High**	**No** (good for a starter Web site or blog but will eventually require a migration)	• In most cases your URL includes the address of the hosting platform (e.g. www.MySite.Blogspot.com) • This leads to the main drawback (and it's a big one) that you don't build up SEO equity to your own URL. By hosting your site on a hosted platform, your SEO equity is passed to the host site (e.g. Blogspot.com). • Often free or expensive
Shopping Cart or Online Store Platform	Self-hosted or hosted versions exist	Depends on the platform – usually **Low** to **Medium**	For adding new products – **High** For adding other content (articles, blog, reviews) – usually **Low**	**Yes** - for companies selling lots of products that need to be managed	• If you need a cart to manage your products and handle sales, then a Shopping Cart platform is for you • A drawback of many Shopping Carts include: • Low ability to do On-page SEO • Often lack of easy way to add keyword-rich content or to integrate a blog

 A CMS which you host yourself is generally the best for both <u>On-page SEO</u> and for <u>adding new content</u> easily

*Some content management systems may offer hosted versions – for better SEO and for maximum flexibility it's recommended that you self-host

Four Popular Content Management Systems for Small and Medium Businesses

- **Wordpress** – www.wordpress.org

    - A very popular open-source platform for both standalone Blogs and Web sites

    - Don't get confused with the hosted platform available from www.Wordpress.com. This is not recommended because all SEO value is passed to Wordpress.com, not to your site or blog.

    - The Wordpress platform is free and you can use it with many hosts (just make sure they advertise compatibility with Wordpress)

    - The look and feel is managed through the use of templates – many free and inexpensive templates are available

    - Advanced functionality can be added using plug-ins (free or paid options exist)

    - On-page SEO can be accomplished fairly easily via the platform combined with specialized plug-ins

    - Wordpress.org's platform is very easy to use compared to other content management systems

- **Three other popular Content Management Systems:**

    - **Joomla** – www.Joomla.org

    - **Drupal** – www.Drupal.org

    - **CMS Made Simple** – www.cmsmadesimple.com

 In addition to these CMS' for small or medium businesses, there are Enterprise-class CMS' for very large companies

---

What to look for in choosing a CMS

☐ Popularity – you want to choose a CMS that is popular because that means developers will continue to improve the platform, templates and plug-ins

☐ Ease of use – try out demos or review training to see if it is easy to use for the people who will be updating your site; the interface should be easy to understand

☐ Contains key functionality that you need for your business (e.g. manages pictures well if you're in the photography business, handles video well if that's important to you, allows you to manage multiple products or integrates with a shopping cart if needed

☐ Allows you to add new functionality via plug-ins or add-ons

☐ Allows you to do the basic On-page SEO tactics including:

- Customizing URLs with keywords; those URLs should be stable over time (not changing dynamically)

- Adding Page Titles and Meta Descriptions

- Adding Alt Tags to pictures

- Adding Headers and Bold or Strong text

- Adding unlimited amounts of content or pages

☐ Should have good documentation, training and support

☐ Allows you to use your own URL and Host

☐ Contains the ability to integrate an analytics platform such as Google Analytics, Piwick or others

Work with someone knowledgeable in both Content Management Systems <u>and</u> SEO when choosing the technology for your Web site

Web Site Structure: Develop logical flow based on how people search; use your keyword clusters

Structure your Web site with the following in mind:

- Usability – help your potential customers navigate your site
- Conversion – make sure you clearly plan for conversions
- SEO – group your pages into related sets of pages that interlink to each other; use Keyword Clusters for each page

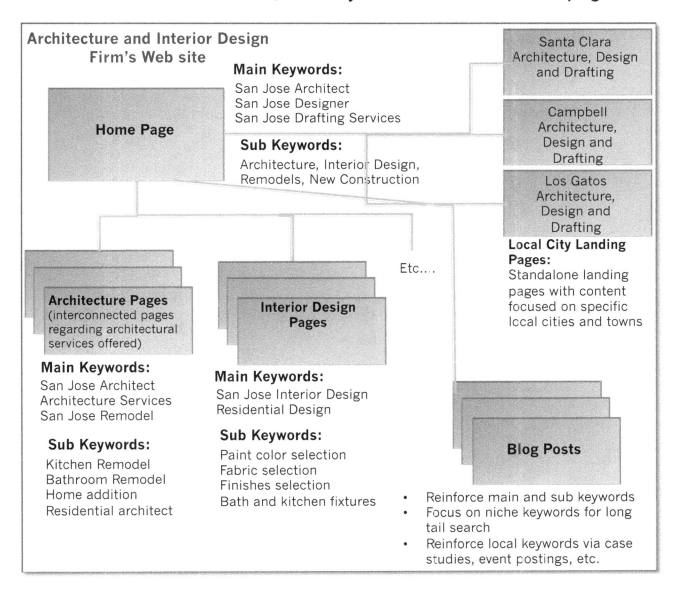

Architecture and Interior Design Firm's Web site

Home Page

Main Keywords:
San Jose Architect
San Jose Designer
San Jose Drafting Services

Sub Keywords:
Architecture, Interior Design, Remodels, New Construction

Santa Clara Architecture, Design and Drafting

Campbell Architecture, Design and Drafting

Los Gatos Architecture, Design and Drafting

Local City Landing Pages:
Standalone landing pages with content focused on specific local cities and towns

Architecture Pages (interconnected pages regarding architectural services offered)

Interior Design Pages

Etc....

Main Keywords:
San Jose Architect
Architecture Services
San Jose Remodel

Sub Keywords:
Kitchen Remodel
Bathroom Remodel
Home addition
Residential architect

Main Keywords:
San Jose Interior Design
Residential Design

Sub Keywords:
Paint color selection
Fabric selection
Finishes selection
Bath and kitchen fixtures

Blog Posts

- Reinforce main and sub keywords
- Focus on niche keywords for long tail search
- Reinforce local keywords via case studies, event postings, etc.

Choose the right domain name

If you're just getting started or have a virtually unvisited Web site, you can consider getting a new domain name

Tips to picking a good domain name:

1. **Short** – easy to pronounce and remember. Passes radio test – if someone heard it on the radio:

   - Can they remember it?
   - Can they spell it correctly?

2. **Compelling** – has some meaning behind it relevant to your company's business

3. **Descriptive** – has elements that help people understand what you do

4. **"dot com"** – for most business Web sites, using ".com" is the best Top Level Domain (TLD)

   - Other TLD's like .Net or .Biz are basically second tier TLDs
   - .Org for non-profits or other organizations
   - .Edu is restricted for educational institutions
   - .TV or .LY or others are a bit of a gimmick but can work in some cases
   - .Au, .De, etc. for sites in Australia or Germany

5. **Keywords** - If possible, include keywords in the URL (can include part or all of the company name if you have a strong brand or would like to brand your company name)

6. **Avoid Acronyms** if possible: People have a hard time remembering acronyms so avoid using them if you can.

 Domain name, Web site technology and other fundamental decisions are hard to reverse later and can negatively impact your SEO and Web strategies – make these decisions very deliberately early on

Don't skimp on Web site hosting service

Google has begun using page load speed in its ranking algorithm. In addition, if your Web site goes offline often this can affect your position in the search results. Google and the other search engines don't want to send their searchers to pages that are not available.

What this means to you:

- Don't skimp on hosting – make sure you go with a solid hosting company

- Look for a host with a good reputation – get a referral or look online at different host rating sites

- **What to look for in a hosting company:**

  - Good up-time

  - Flexible in terms of services and plan

  - Easy-to-use – they use a user-friendly control panel

  - Up-to-date technology

  - Variety of features and add-ons that you can use

  - Compatible with the Web site technology you'll be using

  - Don't discourage you from buying and keeping your domain names at a separate company (you can point them to your host's nameservers)

  - Good customer support reputation

 You Web site host is like the foundation you build your house on. You'll pay later if you go with a discount host that provides low quality and poor service.

A Web site analytics package is essential for tracking SEO progress

Web site analytics are software programs that are usually implemented by adding a small piece of HTML code to your Web site's pages. They capture data on the visits to your site so you can analyze things such as:

- Traffic trends over time
- Numbers of new visitors
- How quickly people leave your site
- How long they stay
- Most visited pages
- Traffic sources
- Keywords used to find your site

A screen shot from Google Analytics

 Not using analytics is like driving a car with a big tarp on the front wind-shield! Don't try it!

Web Analytics Packages

Free Analytics Packages:

There are a couple of great, free products to get many of you started:

- **Google Analytics** is a great free platform used by millions of site owners

  - www.google.com/analytics

- **Piwik** provides an open source alternative to Google Analytics. It takes slightly more technical knowledge to set up, but not much.

  - www.piwik.org

- There are other free or inexpensive analytics packages available but Google Analytics covers the need fairly well

Paid Analytics Packages:

Other packages geared at larger companies include:

- **Webtrends** – www.webtrends.com

- **Omniture** – www.omniture.com

- **Coremetrics** – www.coremetrics.com

Wrap up: Web sites, Domain Names, Hosting and Analytics

In this chapter we covered:

A. **Web site goals, technology and structure**

B. **Domain name and hosting**

C. **Web site analytics**

You should now have a better understanding of the choices you can make with regards to these areas. Some will help your SEO (and marketing) efforts and others may impede them. As many of these topics can get fairly complex for non-techies, make sure you work with your technical group, friend or consultant and use resources (such as Google and Bing searches) to get more details on specific items.

In the next chapter we'll be talking about developing an SEO Balanced Scorecard.

Chapter 5. Developing an SEO Balanced Scorecard

Measuring progress is an essential part of a good SEO strategy

<u>Contents</u>

A. **Balanced scorecard overview**
B. **Specific metrics you can track**
C. **Tools to help you track your metrics**

Develop Scorecard, get baseline metrics and set reporting schedule

In order to track the impact of your SEO strategy you need to follow some key SEO metrics over time as well as some related metrics (i.e. conversions, Social Media promotion success rate, pay-per-click campaign metrics)

This aggregation of metrics is your "SEO Balanced Scorecard". It gives a balanced view of your performance across a variety of different measures. Below are some potential metrics you can use.

- Essential SEO metrics:
    - Search Engine ranking for top 10-20 phrases on Google and Bing (you can track many more but you should at least be aware of the top 10-20)
    - Number of pages indexed in Google and Bing
    - Number and quality of inbound links
    - Web site traffic, visitors, traffic sources, bounce rate, time on site
    - Target conversions and conversion rate

- Other Potential Metrics:
    - Social Media mentions of your site
    - Facebook or Twitter fans/followers
    - YouTube video views
    - Site load speed
    - Online sales
    - Pay-per-click campaign statistics

 It's important to pick key metrics, take a measurement early on (baseline), and then track progress over time

Example of the summary page of an SEO Balanced Scorecard

Illustrative Data

Pages Indexed/Inbound Links

	Last month	This month	% improvement
Pages indexed			
•Google	49	61	19%
•Bing	36	43	21%
•Yahoo	47	51	7%
Inbound Links by PageRank:			
•PR8-10 pages	2	3	50%
•PR5-7 pages	3	5	83%
•PR2-4 pages	12	14	18%
•PR0-1 pages	27	31	11%

Keywords/Ranking

Number of Keyword ranking in:	Last month	This month	Goal / % of goal
Positions 1-10	5	8	10
Positions 11-20	3	6	5
Positions 20-30	7	12	2
Positions 30-40	10	15	16
Positions 40-50	23	25	22
Not ranking in top 50	43	40	36

Website Traffic

	Last month	This month	% improvement
Total Traffic	1,204	1,453	15%
Traffic Sources:			
Search	432	543	11%
Referrals	540	567	2%
Direct	276	285	2%
Avg. time on site	2:34	3:45	23%
Avg pages visited	3.1	3.6	12%
Avg bounce rate	45%	36%	25%

Conversions/Social Media

	Last month	This month	% improvement
Twitter:			
•Tweets	64	75	18%
•Followers	345	465	16%
Facebook:			
• Members	234	245	2%
YouTube:			
•Views	33	23	-35%
Newsletter Subscribers	275	245	-9%
New Leads	7	14	100%
Internet-influenced Sales	$235K	$301K	16%

What gets measured gets done – make sure all key individuals know what you're tracking

PR* = Toolbar PageRank

Pages Indexed:

The number of pages you have indexed in the search engines (mainly Google and Bing since Yahoo and Bing struck a search deal using Bing's search engine). Two things to look out for:

- Are the pages indexed approximately equal to the pages you have on your site (including blog posts)?
- Are you growing your site's footprint on the Internet (and increasing the amount of good keyword-rich content) by growing the total number of pages.
- If your site is not indexed at all, you should make sure it gets submitted.

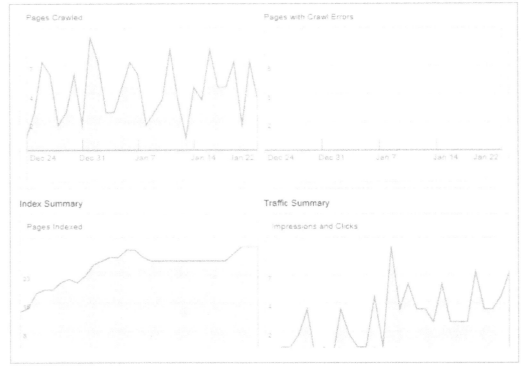

Pages crawled and indexed from Bing Webmaster Center

Tools for Checking Pages Indexed:

- **Google** – www.google.com
    - Enter the following in the search bar: site:MyCompany.com and you can also use site: www.MyCompany.com (no spaces after "site:")
- **Bing** – www.bing.com
    - Enter the same info as above for Google

Go to www.DirectionSEO.com/SEO/SEOTools to learn more about SEO Tool Options

Inbound Links (also called Backlinks):

The number and quality of inbound links to pages on your site:
- Number of links – are you growing the number of links to your pages?
- Are they going to the right pages?
- Are you getting links from quality sites? (a proxy is Google Toolbar PageRank)
- Are they using good anchor text?

Main Link Report

Page URL	Page Rank	Anchor	Link Type	Outbound Links	Link Strength
http://www.furnitureinfashion.net/links/ho	1	Flooring Suppl	Good	42	1
http://www.austinenergyservices.com/re	1	Flooring Suppl	Good	17	2
http://www.calwooddirect.com/	0	-N/A-	Missing	7	1
http://www.simplefloors.com/resources/v	0	Flooring Suppl	Good	79	0
http://wood-direct.com/	0	-N/A-	Missing	7	1
http://www.constructionlounge.com/index	-Not Found-	http://www.ca	No Follow	5	0
http://yellowpages.cbs5.com/san-francis	-Not Found-	-N/A-	Missing	6	0
http://search.10pig.com.cn/esearch.aspx	-Not Found-	-N/A-	Missing	43	0
http://www.zibb.com/All/Search/All?q=w	-Not Found-	-N/A-	Text	1	0
http://local.yahoo.com/results?stx=wood	-Not Found-	-N/A-	Missing	48	0
http://cache.spyfu.com/Default.aspx?d=	-Not Found-	Flooring Suppl	Good	128	0
http://www.relogic.com/Company/home_	-N/A-	Flooring Suppl	Good	17	0
http://www.kitchen-secrets.com/Links40	-N/A-	Flooring Suppl	Good	17	0
http://www.morechinacabinets.com/Rugs	-N/A-	Flooring Suppl	Good	26	0
http://www.paylessboxes.com/web-bo:	-N/A-	Flooring Suppl	Good	2	0
http://www.brass-hardware.com/links/as	-N/A-	Flooring Suppl	Good	15	0

Link Diagnosis screenshot

Tools for Checking Inbound Links:

- **Link Diagnosis** – www.linkdiagnosis.com
    - Plugin for Firefox browser
- **SEO Pro Link Checker** - http://seopro.com.au/free-seo-tools/link-checker/
- **Majestic SEO** – www.majesticseo.com
- **AdGoogroo Link Insight** - http://www.adgooroo.com/
- **SEOMoz Toolbar** (for Chrome browser) - http://www.seomoz.org/seo-toolbar
- **Yahoo! Site Explorer** – https://siteexplorer.search.yahoo.com/mysites
    - Hit explore URL and select "except from this domain"
    - Site Explorer, the popular tool, may be discontinued by Yahoo

Web site Traffic:

Is traffic to your site growing?
- What is the source of the traffic – is it coming from your efforts?
- Are people coming from the right geographies?
- What about the time on site – are people spending more time on your site?
- Is your bounce rate going down? Are people staying as opposed to clicking away immediately (called a bounce)?

Web site analytics tools:

Google Analytics (free) - www.google.com/analytics

Piwik (free) - www.piwik.org

Webtrends – www.webtrends.com

Omniture – www.omniture.com

Coremetrics – www.coremetrics.com

Conversions:

Are you getting more conversions?
- Measure your target conversions per month (or week or day).
- Examples include:
    - People joining your mailing list
    - People signing up for your Twitter or Facebook accounts
    - Downloading a white paper
    - Watching a video
    - Making a purchase
    - Requesting a free consultation

Illustrative Data

Conversions	Jan	Feb	Mar
$'s Sales	$1,750	$3,400	$5,600
Leads generated	1	4	9
Newsletter Sign-ups	21	47	131
Facebook Fans added	5	65	156

You need to set up your conversion measurement based on the different conversions you're trying to get. The sources of these metrics will vary.

Search Engine Rank for target keywords:

Check your rank on Google and Bing for your target keywords.
- Is your rank improving?
- Are there target keywords where you have no rank? Maybe you need to create a landing page for this keyword or make some other adjustments.
- Are you ranking in all of the search engines?

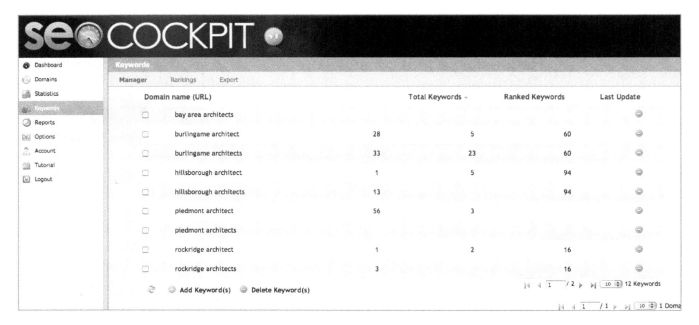

Tools for measuring Search Engine Rankings:

- **SEO Book Rank Checker** (free Firefox plugin)
    - http://tools.seobook.com/firefox/rankchecker/
- **SEO Cockpit** (inexpensive Web-based tool)
    - www.SEOcockpit.com
- **SEOMoz RankTracker** (paid membership required)
    - http://www.seomoz.org/rank-tracker
- **SEO Power Suite – Rank Tracker** (free and paid versions)
    - http://www.link-assistant.com/rank-tracker/

Toolbar PageRank:

While Toolbar PageRank is known to be inaccurate, it can be used as a proxy for Google's view of your authority. Take it with a grain of salt.

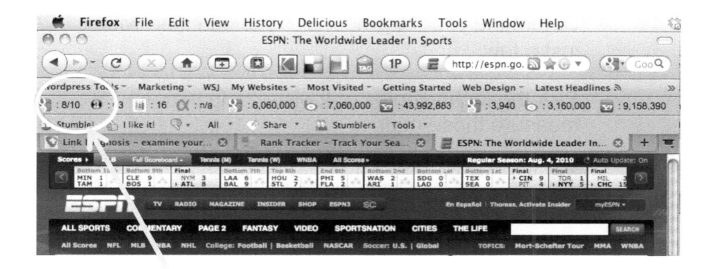

Google Toolbar PageRank (8/10 for the home page of ESPN.com)

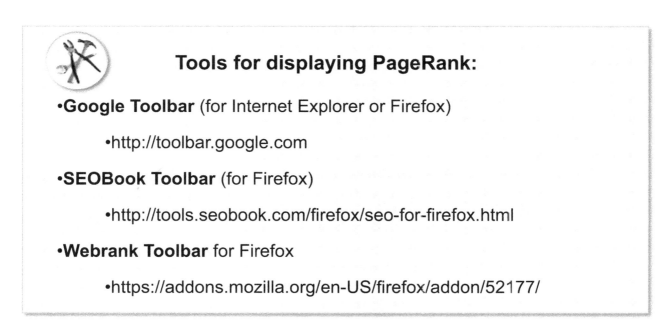

Tools for displaying PageRank:

•**Google Toolbar** (for Internet Explorer or Firefox)

   •http://toolbar.google.com

•**SEOBook Toolbar** (for Firefox)

   •http://tools.seobook.com/firefox/seo-for-firefox.html

•**Webrank Toolbar** for Firefox

   •https://addons.mozilla.org/en-US/firefox/addon/52177/

Wrap-up: Key steps to developing your
SEO Balanced Scorecard

1. Determine your key metrics – you can start with just a few

2. Pick the technologies or tools to help you measure those metrics

3. Set a baseline measurement for each of those metrics

4. Determine who will be the reporting lead and set a schedule for reporting

5. Document the results, communicate the progress to stakeholders and set schedule to recheck

 Using the right measurement and analysis tools is critical to your SEO success. Do your homework but don't worry, there are lots of options – paid and free.

Chapter 6.
19 Essential SEO Concepts Explained

Sending the right signals to the
search engines with on-page and
off-page SEO tactics

Contents

A. **Must-do SEO tactics**

B. **Good-to-do SEO tactics**

C. **Optional SEO tactics**

Additional topics:

- **Anchor Text Explanation**
- **View Source**

It's not essential that you <u>do</u> all of these tactics but it's essential that you <u>understand</u> each

SEO Essentials	Must-Do	Good-To-Do	Optional
1. Attract quality inbound links	☑		
2. Unique page title for all pages	☑		
3. A big helping of keyword-rich textual content	☑		
4. Simple HTML navigation versus (or in addition to) JavaScript or Flash navigation	☑		
5. Use of landing pages 100% focused on 1-3 target keyword phrases	☑		
6. Search Friendly URLs for your Web site	☑		
7 Internal linking in your using good anchor text	☑		
8. 301 Redirects for missing pages or changed URLs	☑		
9. Quality web host with excellent uptime	☑		
10. Create an XML site map and submit it to Google and Bing		☑	
11. Keyword Phrases in header tags and bold/strong		☑	
12. Meta description tags for each page of your Web site		☑	
13. Use video, optimize it and create a video site map		☑	
14. Optimize your files including video, images, PDFs, audio files and presentations		☑	
15, Register your site with Google Webmaster Central and Bing Webmaster Center		☑	
16. Register your site with Google Places and Bing Local		☑	
17. Keywords in domain name			☑
18. Improve page load speed where possible			☑
19. Meta keyword tags on key pages of your Web site			☑

Attract Quality Inbound Links

Must Do!

Overview

The biggest driver of improved search engine rankings is getting quality inbound links from other Web sites pointing to key pages on your site. This is critical if you are trying to achieve Page 1 rankings.

The best way to get links pointing to your site is to have excellent content and publicize it. Other methods include requesting links, having your products/services reviewed, getting PR that leads to online articles, putting links to your site on other sites you own and many other tactics.

SEO value: ★★★★★
Other value: ★★★★☆

SEO Value:
- The #1 factor for ranking in the search engines

Other Value:
- People will follow inbound links, driving traffic to your site this way (in addition to the search engine ranking improvements)
- Quality pages are usually high traffic pages so expect a steady stream of direct visitors from a successful linking campaign

Link quality is higher if:

- The link comes from an authoritative and trustworthy site

- The site, section or page is relevant to your page's topic

- The link is in the content of a page with relevant surrounding keywords

- The link is not a part of a list of "helpful resources" but is part of a Web page's main textual content

- The link is one of a limited number of outbound links on that page

- The link has good, relevant anchor text*

- There is diversity in the anchor text of the links coming to you from different sites (this looks more natural to search engines)

- There is some diversity in types of sites linking to you

- Most or all of the links are one-way (meaning from those sites to your site). Exchanged links may pass less value in the eyes of the search engines.

*See p.88 for more about anchor text

Some of the best ways to get links include (See <u>Chapter 7: Link-Building Essentials </u> for more):

- The best Link-Building tactic is to develop compelling content that compels people to link to your site. Some examples include:
    - Writing an authoritative "how-to" or "top 10 article" that attracts other site owners to write up a brief summary on their own blog and then to link to your article
    - Provide an interactive resource such as a mortgage calculators or calorie counter. Obviously you need to think of some angle that's relevant for your industry that others don't have!
    - Creating a video or slide presentation that is funny, authoritative or educational

- A key part of building links with content is publicizing the content:
    - Utilize Social Media channels (Twitter, Facebook, LinkedIn)
    - Broadcast via a newsletter
    - Make sure it's included in your blog
    - Tell your customers or prospects about it

- Other Link-Building tactics include:
    - A regular series of posts that are authoritative for your industry
    - Submitting your site to trustworthy and authoritative niche directories
    - Finding out where top-ranked sites are getting links from and trying to get links from those sources
    - Writing an article or blog post for a top industry publication or getting them to write about your company or products/services
    - Joining an industry or local organization that includes a link to your site

Common Mistakes:

1. **Paying someone you don't know to get links for you:** These links will be around for a long time. Having "Link Spam" on a variety of low-quality forums, directories and other pages may hurt you as much as it helps!

2. **Link Exchanges:** Participating in a link exchange program with several other sites. Your best links are "one way" links coming from a good site to you, not exchanging with other "average" sites. Spend your energy getting links from "good" sites (even if you get less of them) than trying to collect tons of links from average or bad sites.

3. **Link Farms**: Spammy, junky sites that are merely collections of links are not valuable for SEO and can be harmful if overdone.

4. **Same Anchor Text for many links:** Search engines prefer that your links grow organically versus through strategic link-building campaigns. Diversity in anchor text looks more organic, so mix it up where you can when submitting your site, when requesting a link or asking for anchor text modification.

5. **Writing poor content thinking it will attract links**: Just because you have content about the right topics doesn't mean people will care. If you don't take the time to think about what will really help people and to write it well people may not be interested.

 If you're not finding ways to attract quality inbound links, you're not doing effective SEO

What is Anchor Text?

Google popularized the use of hyperlinks (we'll generally call them "links") as the best way to judge the popularity of Web Pages. But in evaluating links, Google doesn't only look at the fact that there's a link from Web site A to Web site B. They look at which page in Web site A has the link (and is it a popular page?), where on the page the link is coming from (e.g. a list or within the content), what the surrounding keywords are and what's the "anchor text" describing the link?

Anchor Text Example (HTML Link)

Anchor text is the set of words used to describe a link. You can link to the popular tech blog, Techcrunch like this:

- Choice 1: www.techcrunch.com
- Choice 2: Tech Crunch Blog
- Choice 3: A great blog for tech news

All three have the same underlying link (http://www.techcrunch.com) but the anchor text for each is different.

Here's the code for Choice 3:

anchor text

```
<a href="http://www.techcrunch.com/">A great blog for tech news</a>
```

Using the anchor text in Choice #3, you would be passing information about Tech Crunch's home page being a "great blog for tech news. The most meaningful keywords that Google would capture would include

- "blog"
- "tech"
- "news"

What about a picture including a link?

In addition, you may insert a picture of the Tech Crunch logo and want them to click on that. In this case, the picture (the logo) becomes the link. There is still the opportunity to incorporate anchor text with a picture link (and you should).

With pictures, you just need to put the anchor text in the "alt tag" portion of the code for the picture. Unlike anchor text for HTML links, this alt text only visibly shows up if the picture doesn't load or is read out if someone is using Web page reader software designed for the blind or sight-impaired.

Anchor Text Example (HTML Link)

Here's what a picture (Tech Crunch logo) with anchor text (alt text) looks like in code:

```
<a href="http://www.techcrunch.com"><img src="http://
www.directionseo.com/wp-content/uploads/2009/09/techcrunch-logo.png"
alt="A great Web site for tech topics"/></a>
```

anchor text

Decoding the code:

- **a href =** this is the Web Page you're linking to
- **Img src=** this is where the image that will be displayed on your page is located ("image source")
- **alt=** this is the alternative text which acts as "anchor text"

2 Unique Page Title for each page

Overview:

Having unique page titles on each page of your Web site with your target keywords is the second most important factor for SEO. You should include your top keywords (for that page) at the beginning of the title tag. You can optionally include your company name at the end of the title tag.

Google and the other search engines use this title tag as a key indicator of the keywords that your page is relevant for.

In addition, the title tag shows up as the "headline" for your search result in a SERP.

Must Do!

SEO value: ★★★★★
Other value: ★★★★☆

SEO: Page Titles are essential for ranking in search engines – just do it!
Other: In addition to being a key item for ranking, your page titles also show up as the first line in a search result when your Web page comes up in a search engine. Descriptive page titles improve click-through rate by indicating what the page is about.

Example:

1) Page Title location on a Web site:

Complete SEO Tools List | Direction SEO

2) Page Title location on a Search Result:

Complete **SEO Tools List** | Direction SEO

Oct 7, 2010 ... Click on this **list** of over 45 **SEO tools** including all of the great input from the SEO community. Includes keyword research tools, ...

www.directionseo.com/seo-tools/34-seo-tools-the-ultimate-tools-list/ - Cached

(The Page Title is the headline for your search result – it's very important in terms of getting searchers to click to your site instead of the other search results that come up)

Code Example:

This is what the Page Title code looks like on your Web page:

```
<title>Tae Kwon Do, Karate and Martial Arts in Pacific Beach, California</title>
```

Details:

- Put primary target keywords for that page at or near the beginning of the title

- Should be located in header section (near the top) of HTML code

- Shoot for around 70 characters (Google's search results include the first 70 characters)

- One unique title for each page on your Web site

- You can optionally put your company name in the Title in addition to target keywords – at the end preferably unless it's a well-known brand

---

Common Mistakes:

1. **Going Generic**: Using generic words such as "Home", "Index", "Contact", or "About Us" as page titles – how will a search engine differentiate your site?

2. **Chapter 1, Chapter 1, Chapter 1…**: All of your pages having the same title - e.g. "ACME Dynamite Company" – that's like naming every chapter of a book the same thing.

3. **No stuffing!** Don't "keyword stuff" your title tags or other tags. Don't repeat your keywords over and over in a way that's annoying to potential visitors and the search engines

---

 Unique Page Titles including your target keywords are essential for SEO. Put this high on your priority list.

Based on their home page Title Tag what do you think the Wall Street Journal's target keywords are?

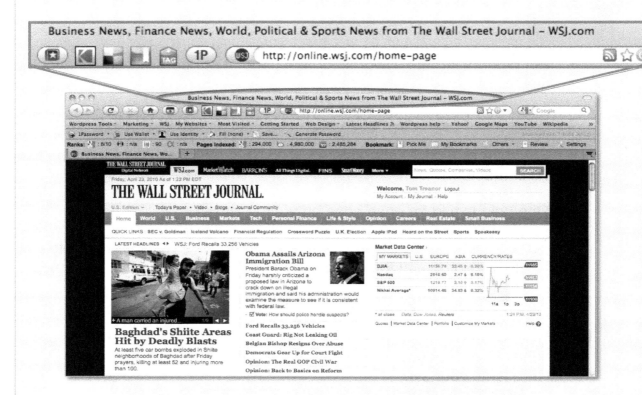

WSJ target keywords appear to be:

Main Keywords:

#1: **Business News**
#2: **Finance News**
#3: **World News**

Secondary Keywords:

#4: Political News
#5: Sports News
#6: Wall Street Journal
#7: WSJ.com

Notice that they don't put "Business, Finance and World News". They instead keep "Business News", "Finance News" and "World News" together as 2-word phrases

3 A big helping of Keyword-rich textual content

Overview

In order to assess Web sites and Web pages in an automated way, search engines read the text on the site and, based on their algorithms, make assessments about the relevance of your site for various keyword phrases. This, combined with the link analysis, and good use of page titles are major factors for deciding how a page will rank in the search engines.

So, clearly the textual content on your site is a key signal for search engines. Your content actually serves three purposes for you:

1) Inform, entertain and build trust with your audience

2) Signal to search engines what your site (and its sections and pages) is about

3) Compel other sites to link to you because your content is so great

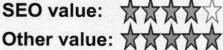

Must Do!

SEO value: ★★★★☆
Other value: ★★★★★

SEO Value:
• Quality content is extremely important for SEO – it provides signals to search engines about your site. It also can attract inbound links which helps with rankings too

Other Value:
• Your customers will appreciate quality content, stay on your site longer and visit more often
• Blogs and other sites will link to quality resources, articles, tools, video or other content

How can search engines possibly differentiate sites based on their use of text? Here are different ways keywords and keyword phrases can be included in your site which will be evaluated by search engines:
• Where it's located (e.g. page titles, headers, within the body, in lists, etc.)
• How often it's repeated
• Use of stemming (e.g. swim, swimming, swimmer)
• Use of synonyms and similar words (e.g. backstroke, breast stroke, wading, paddling)
• Use keywords in the anchor text of links
• Use in meta title and meta description tags
• Number of keyword phrase repetitions compared to other words on a page (keyword density)
• What section of your Web site it's in and are the pages in that section related to the same or similar topics?
• Use of keywords in video, audio, presentation or document file names
• Use of keywords in picture alt tags

Details:

What are some guidelines for creating content?

- Write for your audience primarily but keep the need for keyword phrases (including stemming and synonyms) in mind as you write or re-write.

- Create self-contained sections in your Web site for pages related to the same or similar content. Link between these similar pages with relevant anchor text.

- Use keywords appropriately in your page titles, headers, bold tags, picture alt tags, title and description meta tags.

- Try to have a minimum of 200 words per page up 400 or so if needed for your topic. If the concepts become complex or different enough, create more pages.

Common Mistakes:

1. **Don't be brief:** Be more descriptive and specific. Use your keywords and synonyms in your content.

2. **Be Unique**: Don't use the same content that other sites have. For example, rewrite product descriptions in order to stand out and to be found by search engines.

3. **Use Keyword Clusters consciously in your pages, sections and content:** Certain pages or areas of your site should be devoted to certain topics (and keyword clusters). Don't mix several topics (and keyword clusters) in one area except with some exceptions (e.g. Home Page).

4. **Don't try to be fancy and invent new words to stand out:** Use the words your customers use, not words that no one will search for.

5. **Using text in pictures or Flash**: Text in pictures or in Flash will generally not be read by search engines. Make sure the majority of your text content is in plain HTML text.

6. **Making it hard to share:** Make sure you provide easy ways for people to share on Facebook, Twitter, email, etc.

 If you're not big on writing or saying much you'll need to force yourself to be more descriptive when you write your Web copy. After time, it becomes more natural.

4 Simple HTML navigation versus (or in addition to) Javascript or Flash navigation

Must Do!

Your site's navigation is the set of links, buttons or menus used to move around your site. Many sites use Javascript or Flash for navigation. Since Search Engines can't reliably crawl Javascript and can't read Flash, it's important that you have simple HTML navigation to your key pages including main topic pages, key landing pages, major resources or other significant pages.

Generally if you click on a menu and more options appear, this is powered by Javascript. If your site has a lot of fancy visuals and, when moving from page to page, the URL doesn't change, this may be a Flash site. Check with your Web developer if you're not sure.

It's fine to use pictures as links with alt tags as anchor text. A search engine can follow this.

SEO value: ★★★★☆
Other value: ★★☆☆☆

SEO Value: This helps the Search Engines spider the key pages in your site.
Other Value: Some people may appreciate using simple text-based navigation.

Code Example: A simple HTML link:

```
<a href='http://www.example.com/services'>Example.com's services portfolio</a>
```

Common Mistakes:

1. **Only Javascript navigation:** Search engines have some trouble following JavaScript navigation

2. **Only Flash navigation:** Search engines can't reliably follow Flash navigation

 If you have Flash or Javascript navigation, make sure to also add HTML navigation that the search engines can easily follow

5 Search Friendly URLs for your Web site

Must Do!

Overview:

Simple, logical, keyword-rich, short, and stable URLs (Web page addresses) are best for both search engines, potential visitors to your site and for people who want to share your URL with others. They are easily read and and indexed by Search Engine spiders because they don't contain extra information that can confuse them. They can lead to increased click-through for your pages when they come up in the search results because searchers will see a nice, simple address. They are easier to share because they're easy to copy, won't get cut in half in emails and stay the same over time (stable).

URLs that contain many parameters, session IDs or meaningless combinations of symbols, numbers and text are harder for search engines to properly spider and index (see examples below). In addition, URLs that are long and confusing are very hard for people to share as well.

Also, URLs that are too many levels deep – about four levels deep (separated by each "/") is the most – run the risk of not being thoroughly crawled and indexed by search engines.

SEO value: ★★★★☆
Other value: ★★★★☆

SEO value: If the Search Engines can't easily index your pages, you can't rank well.
Other value: Short, easy to read and stable URLs are more helpful for sharing and linking

Example:

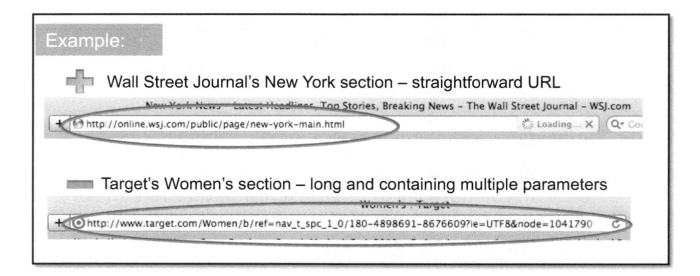

+ Wall Street Journal's New York section – straightforward URL

New York News – Latest Headlines, Top Stories, Breaking News – The Wall Street Journal – WSJ.com
http://online.wsj.com/public/page/new-york-main.html   Loading... ✕   Go

▬ Target's Women's section – long and containing multiple parameters

Women's : Target
http://www.target.com/Women/b/ref=nav_t_spc_1_0/180-4898691-8676609?ie=UTF8&node=1041790

Details:

- Simple, logical, straightforward URLs (ideally with your target keywords) are much better for getting your pages properly indexed by the search engines

- For your main pages, find a way to create fixed, simple and keyword-rich URLs. Content management systems like Wordpress.org (self-hosted version) allow you to customize your URLs to be more search engine friendly.

Common Mistakes:

1. **Multiple parameters and code making URLs long and unreadable**: Multiple parameters, tracking code and long URLs lead to clipped URLs in email, difficulty for search engines to crawl and index, and make it less likely that people will share your URL.

2. **Same URL for all pages**: A static URL for your site which stays the same even when you navigate to other pages. A company I worked with had a static URL (which was the same no matter which page I was on). I couldn't share the price list or map page with anyone because there was no unique address for any page!

3. **Dynamically-generated URLs that change (no stable URL)**: Dynamically-generated URLs that are different each time for the same page make it impossible to index and hard for people to find that page again or link to it.

4. **Spaces or underlines in the URL:** Ideally you shouldn't use spaces or underlines in a URL because nonsense symbols will be used in the URL in place of a space and underline is not recognized as a space. Dashes ("-") are better than underlines – they are considered a space by a search engine.

 Short, user-friendly URLs are better for searchers, search engines and people who want to share or link to your Web pages

6 Use of <u>Landing Pages</u> 100% focused on 2-4 main target keyword phrases

Must Do!

Landing pages are pages on your Web site dedicated to a limited number of keyword phrases and to a specific audience and/or offer. They should be highly targeted towards certain keyword phrases in all aspects – page title, page description, headers and content. Also, if you can get quality inbound links pointing at your key landing pages, these landing pages will rank higher in the search engines.

Developing focused landing pages can be time-intensive but is a key way of breaking from the pack in SEO.

SEO value: ★★★★☆
Other value: ★★★★★

SEO value: Allows you to optimize the on-page SEO very tightly around target keywords. Also allows you to focus on getting targeted inbound links as well.
Other value: Results in Web pages that attract searchers for very targeted keywords. Leads to higher conversion rate. Also, these can be very useful for PPC campaigns.

Details:

- Make sure you pick on the main and supporting keywords you'll be focusing on. This should be one of the Keyword Clusters from Chapter 3.

- Pick the audience you're targeting for this page.

- Make sure you optimize the URL, the page title, the page description, the header tags and the content.

- Pick content that will be compelling to the visitors.

- Determine the next steps you want them to take after getting to this landing page. Are you trying to get a conversion on this page or move them to another page on your site?

 Spending the time to create landing pages that focus on specific target customers, use keyword clusters, are optimized for SEO and that have a defined "next step" should be a key part of your SEO strategy

7 Internal linking in your using good anchor text

Must Do!

Internal Linking:

Within your content, you should link to other content on your site with appropriate anchor text. This helps you move "link juice" to key pages (of your choice) within your site. They also provide a way for your readers to discover other pages or resources on your site. Some things to consider related to internal linking:

- Links from the home page carry a lot of weight – you can link to your highest priority landing pages

- Interlink to other pages on similar topics to clearly communicate to search engines about the contents of your site

- Put links within your content (e.g. within a paragraph) versus in a list. This gives higher SEO value to the page being linked to

- Use anchor text to pass more information to the search engines

SEO value: ★★★★☆
Other value: ★★★☆☆

SEO Value: Proper inter-linking is very good for your SEO.

Other Value: Internal Linking in your site can help your visitors find your other content and stay on your site. Linking out appropriately generates good will and is good Web etiquette.

Use anchor text:

The anchor text in your links as well as the text surrounding a link can communicate to search engines (and your users) the topic of the link.

Focus your inbound links to the pages you want to push up in ranking for a particular topic

Common Mistakes:

1. **Not cross-linking within your site:** For search engines and people, make sure you have links within your site to other related pages.

2. **Being afraid to link out**: Linking out to other sites is the common practice on the Internet. Don't be afraid to link to useful resources or authorities in the industry where appropriate.

3. **Linking across major sections of your Web site:** On your site, keep the links across pages with similar content – hopefully those pages are also in the same section.

4. **Taking people away from your site on key conversion pages:** One exception to the outbound linking principles. Try not to have a major link that takes people away from your site on your key conversion pages.

Related Topic - Linking Out:

On a related note, it's good to link out to relevant authority or helpful sites within your content. First of all, it's good etiquette to link to sources you might refer to in the course of an article or blog post. Second, your "in-context" links can be valuable to other sites. So, you'll generate some goodwill with strategic linking out – who knows, maybe they'll provide links back to you at some point as well. Third, Google's algorithm may include external linking to authority sites (with appropriate anchor text) as one of its components in determining which keywords your site is focused on.

 Linking to authority sites is not a bad thing to do. Give credit where credit is due by linking to sites you reference

8 **301 Redirects** for missing pages or changed URLs

Must Do!

If your URLs change, if your pages are deleted or if you change to a new domain name, there will be pages that search engines will have indexed but that now lead to a non-existent page. Or Web sites will have links pointing to pages of your site that no longer exist. These are called broken links.

You should do a 301 redirect any time you know there is a missing page or changed URL. If you register your site with Google Webmaster tools, they will highlight broken links.

SEO value: ★★★☆☆
Other value: ★★★☆☆

SEO value: 301 passes "link juice" and seamlessly directs search engines or people to a new page. This helps preserve any SEO value that existed on the old page.

Other value: 301 redirects make a better experience for everyone involved – your visitors, Webmasters linking to you and the search engines.

Details:

301 Redirects are usually taken care of in a file called htaccess. Work with your Web developer or Web host to do 301 redirects for your site.

Common Mistakes:

1. **Changing a domain name but not 301'ing the old one**: You can 301 direct an entire site. Make sure you do this to let the search engines know that the Web site has been replaced. Also, searchers who land on the old site will instantly be redirected to the new one.

2. **Changing or Deleting a Web page but not 301'ing the old one to the new one:** 301 redirects allow links, search engines and visitors to be redirected seamlessly.

 Do 301 redirects – especially for key pages that go missing or get changed

9 Quality Web Host with excellent uptime Must Do!

It's important that your Web site loads quickly and is available when people want to visit it. In fact, Google announced that it's officially including page load speed as a factor in its search ranking algorithm.

Your host is a key part of that equation. A quality Web host uses newer servers, solid technology and redundancy to make sure that your site is up when it needs to be and that performance is optimal.

Don't go cheap when looking for a Web host.

SEO value: ★★☆☆☆
Other value: ★★★☆☆

SEO value:
- Google uses load time and uptime as factors in ranking sites – quality hosting can make sure your site is available and as quick as possible.

Other value:
- It's very frustrating to have a site load slowly or be down often. People won't come back a second time.
- In addition, good hosts have robust control panels with lots of options that save you time and effort.

Common Mistakes:

Getting the cheapest host possible: Don't hurt your site's usability by being pennywise and pound-foolish.

Resources:

- If you search on the internet for "Web Hosting Ratings" you can find various rating sites for hosts – including uptime, ratings and prices
- We run our sites on Bluehost.com and are an affiliate via the following link: (http://www.BlueHost.Com/track/RMM). I like Bluehost's easy integration with Wordpress.

Don't go ultra-cheap on your hosting – it may hurt you in the end and make things harder for you

10 Create an XML site map and submit it to Google and Bing

Good to Do!

An XML site map is different than what you might find in the "Site Map" section of a Web site. Typically the site map on a Web site is a set of HTML links designed to help users (or search engines) quickly discover key pages on the site.

An XML site map is a site map created using a special format (XML). It is not designed to be seen by your Web visitors.

After it's created and posted in a particular location on your Web site, you then submit it to Google and Bing.

SEO value: ★★★☆☆
Other value: ★☆☆☆☆

SEO value: This provides the most value for new sites or sites that have added a lot of pages or content. Submitting when there are changes or additions makes sure your pages are in the indexes (which helps you be found).
Other value: Being properly indexed by the search engines is the main value of XML site maps.

XML sitemaps make sure that all of your Web pages get crawled effectively by the search engines. If your sitemap changes, it can be resubmitted to help the search engines quickly discover the changes.

Wordpress (self-hosted version) has plugins for creating XML sitemaps and automatically submitting them to the search engines as they get updated.

Resources:

- For help in creating an XML sitemap: http://www.sitemaps.org/
- Submit sitemap via Google Webmaster Central: http://www.google.com/places/
- Submit sitemap via Bing Webmaster Center: https://ssl.bing.com/listings/ListingCenter.aspx

 An XML site map helps the search engines keep track of and index the pages of your site. If your site is already well-indexed by the search engines there won't be a boost. But if your site is not well-indexed, this can help you quite a bit

11 <u>Keyword Phrases</u> in Header Tags and Bold/Strong

Good to Do!

Overview

On a Web page, the formatting can include normal text and a variety of headers (see below for examples), as well as "bold" or "strong" formats.

In the past, the keywords that were in headers as well as in bold or strong tags were considered to be key signals to the search engines. This has diminished as link-based signals have become much more important.

SEO value: ★★☆☆☆
Other value: ★★☆☆☆

SEO Value: Generally considered to have just a small amount of value in terms of getting ranked in search engines
Other Value: Well-organized sites with good, descriptive headers and bold at the right places may help your readers

Because they may still provide some signals to the search engines, you should still be aware of what keywords you put in your Headers and in bold (or strong) when you create your content. The priority would be Header 1 first, Header 2 next and bold or strong next. Headers 3-6 are optional or can be ignored. You should have only one H1 tag on any given page (if possible).

Examples:	Code Examples:
# This is Header 1	`<h1>This is Header 1</h1>`
## This is Header 2	`<h2>This is Header 2<h2>`
This is Bold Text	`<bold>This is Bold Text</bold>`
This is Strong Text	`<strong>This is Strong Text</strong>`

Common Mistakes:

1. **Using H1, H2 or Bold/Strong tags without any target keywords:** Don't over-do it but instead of saying "About Us", why not say "About XYZ Consulting" or instead of "Our 5 Step Process" you can say, "Our 5 Step Strategic Consulting Process"

2. **Using too many H1, H2 and bold phrases so the page is confusing for users**: Focus most on H1 and maybe some H2 and bold or strong. Keep the pages fairly clean and organized.

3. **Not using any H1, H2 or bold phrases:** Don't just have straight text with no headers or emphasis anywhere. Your readers at least will appreciate it!

4. **Writing for search engines and not your readers:** Be conscious of SEO for your site structure and in your content development. When you actually write, make sure the writing is engaging and makes sense for your readers.

5. **Keyword-stuffing Headers and Bold/Strong:** Don't overstuff your headers or bold/strong tags with keywords!

 Generally what can be gamed easily loses its SEO value over time – that's why header tags have become less valuable and why meta keyword tags have little to no SEO value

What is a meta tag?

Meta tags are specific fields put into the code of Web sites that are designed to be read by search engines spiders. They crawl the internet to index the web pages they find. Meta tags are generally not visible to users (with some exceptions).

Types of Meta Tags include:

- Meta keywords tag – formerly used by search engines to determine a Web page's main keywords. No longer important for search engines.

- Meta description tag – a tag that allows for a description of each page of your Web site. This is only seen by users when all or part of it is used in lines 2 and 3 of a search result.

- Meta robots tag – indicates whether or not you want the search engines to include a specific page in their index. In some cases you don't want them to include your pages in the index (e.g. login pages or private but not password-protected pages). In this case you would tell the search engines not to index the page using the meta robots tag.

Meta Tags are typically placed in the Header Section of the code of a Web page. Some content management systems (CMS) such as Wordpress (self-hosted version) and Joomla allow you to easily fill in these tags (plugins may be needed). These meta tags can easily be placed in the Header section of an HTML page by your Webmaster.

12 Meta Description Tags for key pages of your Web site

Good to Do!

Meta description tags are descriptions of what your page is about and why someone should be interested (and click on it). It is often used by search engines for use as the page description in a SERP.

It is not considered a major factor for SEO but it is important for attracting visitors because a good search result listing (see below) will help get searchers to click more often on your link versus others on the Search Engine Results Page (SERP).

SEO value: ★★☆☆☆
Other value: ★★★★☆

SEO value: Because there is potential to game meta description tags with keywords they are generally not considered major factors for ranking.
Other value: Meta Description Tags are very valuable though because they are often used in the SERP as the 2 line description of your Web page (under the Title). A compelling description can be key in getting people to click your link over someone else's link.

Example:

Video Editing Software, Video Capture Software and Video Creation Services
Acme Video is the nation's largest distributor and wholesaler of **video editing** and **video** capture software. We also provide **video** creation and consulting **services**.
www.AcmeVideo.com/ - Cached

This 2 line "snippet" in a search result will often be based on your Meta Page Description. If you don't have a Meta Description tag, search engines will often pull content from your Web page to create the snippet. It's better to put the message you want than to leave it to chance! The search terms (in this case "video editing services") are highlighted in the snippet.

Code Example:

```
<meta name="description" content="Acme Video is the nation's largest distributor and wholesaler of video editing and video capture software. We also provide video creation and consulting services." />
```

Details:

- Where: In header tag after page title
- What: This is basically marketing copy – make it compelling and include your keywords
- Length: Shoot for about 160 characters
- Keywords: Include the main keywords for that page in sentence format

---

Common Mistakes:

1. **Keyword stuffing**: Repeating the same or similar keywords multiple times.

2. **Not creating a Meta Description Tag for all of your key pages**: This is a great chance to determine what searchers will see when you come up in the results. Don't pass up that opportunity!

3. **Too short or too long:** About 160 characters is the right length for a Meta Description Tag.

The meta page description should be good marketing copy that will be seen in Search Engine Results Pages (SERPs). It's very important to write a good description for your key pages.

Using "view source" to look at your web code (or others)

Do you ever want to check to see whether your Web developer has put in a meta description tag or alt tags for pictures? You may want to. The more you know about your own site, the more you can work with your Web developer to meet your goals.

Did you ever want to see what keywords a competitor was focusing on or how they implemented that cool feature or their Web site?

To do both of these things you probably should get to know the "view source" function that comes with your web browser. This is one of the essential tools to quickly take a glance the code on a Web page. Here's how you get to it in different web browsers. On the menu at the top of the browser start with "View".

- Internet Explorer: View > Source
- Safari: View > Source
- Firefox: View > Page Source
- Chrome: View > Developer > View Source

Once you're looking at the code with view source, you can scan it for what you want or you can go to the "Find" function within your browser's menu and type in "description", "meta", "alt" or other keywords depending on what you're looking for.

13 Use video, optimize it and create a video site map

All of the search engines are increasingly moving towards "Universal Search". This means that they are trying to include more diverse types of content in the results – links to relevant pages, videos, pictures, news stories, Social Media content, files and more.

SEO value: ★★★☆☆
Other value: ★★★★☆

SEO value: Well-optimized video has some advantages for SEO over other types of content so take advantage of this opportunity.
Other value: Video can liven up your site, make your products/service and their benefits come alive and can provide a more personal and compelling approach to getting the word out.

Video is harder, more expensive, and harder to optimize than basic written content. Due to this, there's an opportunity to get your video to rank in search engines for your target keyword phrases. This is especially true for niche topics that aren't well-covered yet.

The other beauty of video is that it really interests a large portion of users. Some people love to read, some people like a mix of reading and video and some people will always go to any video content first. By bringing in video, you're really unlocking a whole new set of customers and making your message more visual, compelling and personal (as you let people see your employees or customers in action).

Details:

- Make sure you have keywords in the file name for your video (use dashes in-between words)
- Add some keyword-rich content in the text before and after the video
- If you post your video on Youtube or other sharing sites make sure you put the URL of your site and your phone number early in the video description.

- Include your site's URL and your contact information in the actual video.

- You should also post the video directly on your site separately from YouTube or any other video sharing service.

- For best optimization, create a video site map and submit it to Google Webmaster Central.

- For information on creating video sitemaps:

  - http://www.google.com/support/webmasters/bin/answer.py?hl=en&answer=80472

Common Mistakes:

1. **Only posting your video on YouTube:** Any links directed to your video on YouTube give more link juice to YouTube. Posting the video directly on your site (and getting links) will provide your site with link juice.

2. **Being afraid to move to video:** Don't be afraid, just give it a try by making at least one video.

3. **Not optimizing the video and the content around the video:** Make sure you optimize the filename, any video metadata and the text on the same page as the video.

4. **Not creating a video sitemap:** It takes a little more effort but it can pay off with good ranking – especially for niche topics.

5. **Making it hard to share:** Make sure you provide an easy way for people to share your video content on Facebook, Twitter and email.

 Video is a great way to rank in the search engines for your target keyword phrases. Also, you unlock a whole new set of customers who prefer video.

14 Optimize your files including Video, Images, PDFs, Audio Files and Powerpoint documents

Good to Do!

It's good SEO practice to optimize files that you put up on your site. This provides more opportunities for your files to come up in searches and reinforces your keywords with the search engines.

File optimization includes things such as using file names containing keywords, each file having a unique name (e.g. if you bought a picture, change the name), making sure the text surrounding them contains relevant information and more. Learn about the basics of file optimization below.

SEO value: ★★★☆☆
Other value: ★★☆☆☆

SEO value: Optimizing files gives them much more of a chance to come up in search results, especially as Universal Search continues to be the norm.
Other value: More information and better (more descriptive) information can only help your visitors (but don't "keyword stuff").

Details:

The basics of file optimization:

- File names should be descriptive
- File names can have dashes but avoid underlines or spaces
- Links to files should have good anchor text, not "click here"
- You should have ample text around your files and it should include relevant keywords
- If an image, the "alt text" should have descriptive keywords (but don't keyword stuff!). If you use an image as a link, remember that your alt text becomes the anchor text
- Rename any files you get from elsewhere – otherwise yours is just one of many of the same. If you rename a file, it becomes unique!

Common Mistakes:

1. **Keeping the file name the same even if you got it from elsewhere:** This won't help you at all as it will be one of many (most likely) on the Internet. Change your file name to a different, descriptive one.

2. **Keeping a picture file name straight from the camera:** A file name like PIC0045678.jpg doesn't have any keywords in it.

3. **Not including descriptive information on the same page as your files:** You need to summarize your files or provide very descriptive, keyword-rich details. In fact, if it's a PDF, video or audio, consider putting the full text on your Web site! There are transcription services that can inexpensively capture all of the text from audio or video.

4. **Not including alt text in picture links:** Remember, the alt text becomes anchor text for picture links.

5. **Not making your files easy to share:** Put sharing buttons near files that you want people to share.

6. **Hiding content behind sign-in forms:** Search engines can't get behind sign-in forms to spider your content. You'll deter a lot of visitors as well.

 Make optimizing your files a standard part of your day-to-day Web design and it won't be a chore

15 Register your site with Google Webmaster Central and Bing Webmaster Center

Good to Do!*

Both Google and Bing provide means to register your sites, to communicate directly to them about your sites and to access free tools to improve the workings of your site.

Although this currently may have limited SEO value now, I think this is low-hanging fruit and will provide you with future opportunities to optimize your site for the search engines. Also, search engines prefer sites that are "verified" and this helps confirm to them that your site is not fly-by-night.

SEO value: ★★☆☆☆
Other value: ★★★☆☆

SEO value: Low to medium SEO value

Other value:
- Allows you to validate your site with the two major search engines.
- Provides some helpful tools and information
- Allows you to get feedback from the search engines

Google's Webmaster Central offers a variety of great tools to help improve your Web site. These include:
- XML site map submission and status – the ability to submit XML sitemaps to the search engines (including special video sitemaps)
- Basic traffic stats (but Google Analytics is much better), top keywords used to find your site, broken links, missing pages
- Inbound link information, HTML suggestions, crawl errors, malware alerts

Bing's Webmaster Center has less tools but Microsoft is aggressively chasing Google and will no doubt develop additional, value-added tools

Resources:

Google Webmaster Central: http://www.google.com/webmasters/
Bing Webmaster Center: http://www.bing.com/webmaster

Registering lets you communicate directly to Google and Bing, allows you to get feedback on your site and also provides you with some helpful tools

*If your pages are not indexed in the search engines this becomes a "must do"

16

Register your site with Google Places and Bing Local

Good to Do!*

Local Search has become an important way for locally-focused businesses to be found on the Internet. Local search is accessed through the standard search interfaces of Google, Bing or Yahoo. Any search that the engine's determine is "local" will include local results which can include maps, addresses, phone numbers, customer reviews and more.

Confirming or adding a local listing is low-hanging fruit, especially for local businesses. It's easy to do and provides more ways to be found online.

SEO value: ★★★★☆

Other value: ★★★☆☆

SEO value: A keyword-rich local listing can help your site be found for local searches.

Other value: Local listings can provide a lot of information to your customers without the need to click through to your site.

Example listings based on Google Places

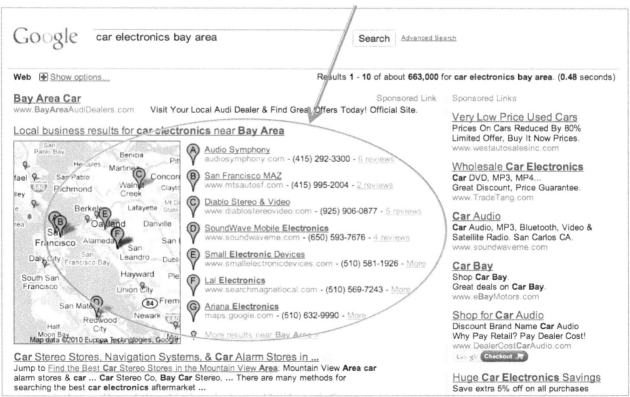

*"Must Do" for Local Business – recommended for others as well

115

The local listings provide an opportunity to:

- Verify your site and physical location with the Google and Bing
- Add pictures, video, business hours, contact information and map location
- Have more chance to rank in local search results
- Add a business and service area even if it is home-based or doesn't have a physical location

Resources:

Google Places: http://www.google.com/local/add/BusinessCenter

Bing Local: https://ssl.bing.com/listings/ListingCenter.aspx

Common Mistakes:

1. **Not owning your listings in Google Places or Bing Local:** It's a big opportunity lost not to claim your business listing in the local sites. Many times the listing is there but the owners have not taken possession. By not claiming your site you're losing the opportunity to put in keyword-rich and informative content.

2. **Not completely filling in your local listing:** Fill it in and make sure the keywords you're focusing on for the rest of your SEO are used here.

3. **Not adding logos, pictures and video:** This is a great opportunity to put additional content that is attractive to users as well as to potentially give you a boost with the search engines.

4. **Not adding your business even if you don't have a storefront**: If you're a consultant, plumber, architect or accountant who works on the phone or at client sites you can still put in a local listing and hide your address.

5. **Not putting in or claiming all of your locations:** Make sure each store location has a separate listing.

 Owning and adding content to a Local Business Listing is low-hanging fruit for Local SEO.
If you're a local only business, this is a must-do

*Must do for Local Business – recommended for others as well

17 Keywords in Domain Name

Optional

Overview

If you're starting a new company or have the flexibility to change your domain name, there is some SEO value in having a major keyword in your domain name.

If your site already has an established following, good traffic or lots of inbound links pointing to it, you might not want to change your domain name. If your domain name includes your company branding and your current domain is very short and memorable, you may not want to change your domain name.

SEO value: ★★☆☆☆
Other value: ★★★☆☆

SEO Value:
- Generally considered to be helpful for SEO to have a keyword in the URL

Other Value:
- Keywords in URL will be bolded in search results if they match the search term
- People may click on a site that has their search term in the URL
- The search term may become the anchor text for an inbound link to your site in some cases

In addition to potentially being valued by search engines, why else would I want a keyword in the domain?

- If your site comes up in a search, any keywords (including those in URLs) that match the search will be displayed in the SERPs in bold

- People may consider Web sites with very relevant terms in their URL to be more authoritative – this could increase your click-through rate

- If people link to your Web site without specifying anchor text, the URL itself may become the anchor text and the keywords in the URL indicate the subject to the Search Engines (possibly helping with ranking)

- Your new name may be more memorable or meaningful to your potential customers

Details:

- Use keywords if possible in your domain name but it's not absolutely essential for SEO

- Short, easy-to-remember and easy-to-spell domain names are best

- Use the most popular Top Level Domain extensions if possible: .com, .org, or .edu TLD's if possible

- Domain names can be purchased on the secondary market – in some cases this can be a good investment

Common Mistakes:

1. **The Radio Test...**": Easy to misspell names don't pass the "radio test". Can people who hear your Web site address spell it correctly?

2. **Morse Code?** Dashes can be used in URLs but it's preferable not to have names with lots of dashes. Which is better to you?

   - DogPottyTraining.com
   - Dog-Potty-Training.com

3. **Looooonnngggg URLs!** Keep it short if possible. Who likes this?

   - DogPottyTrainingSanFrancisco.com

4. **Too easily giving up on finding the right TLD (usually ".com"):**

   People will use and remember URLs with ".com" at the end so try to use it if possible. Here are some ideas about common Top Level Domains:

   - .com for most uses, including business and personal
   - .net is similar but a second choice
   - .org for organizations (non-profits, clubs, associations)
   - .edu for schools
   - .cn, .fr, etc. for Chinese sites, French sites, etc.

5. **Forgetting to redirect your old URL:** If you do change your URL, don't forget to do a 301 for your whole site! This transfers people going to the old address and the search engines will pass the SEO value from the old site to the new site.

 If you're starting from scratch or have a poor domain name now, make efforts to find a better name with keywords in it. If you already have an established brand or Web site, it's more difficult to change.

18 Meta Keyword Tags on key pages of your Web site

Years ago, meta keyword tags were a ranking factor for search engines. The keywords found in that tag helped search engines determine what keywords your site should rank for.

Of course, it's so easy to stuff the meta keywords tag that it became less useful for search engines and one-by-one, they stated that they don't use them for ranking.

Optional

| SEO value: | ★☆☆☆☆ |
| Other value: | ★☆☆☆☆ |

SEO value: Not officially used by search engines but some anecdotal stories about it having minor impact.

Other value: Not Much!

It's not necessary to use the Meta Keywords Tag. Some reasons people do use it:

- There is no penalty for putting keywords in the meta keywords tag.

- Insurance in case things change, in case they are used in some rare situation or in case a smaller search engine picks up on your meta keywords.

- Anecdotal evidence that sites with only meta keywords tag changes have had minor ranking impacts (take this with a grain of salt!).

- It helps keep them organized – they use meta keywords tag to help you keep their target keywords for each page straight.

- They use this for misspellings or other versions of keywords that they couldn't get onto the page (e.g. synonyms or stemming).

- Many people think (wrongly) that this is what SEO is all about!

Code Example;

```
<meta name="keywords" content="search engine marketing, internet
marketing, Web site design, SEM, search engine optimization, SEO,
consulting, domain name, small business, Burlingame, San Mateo, Palo
Alto" />
```

Common Mistakes:

1. **Spending too much time on meta keyword tags:** You should use the keywords from your keyword research. Don't waste a lot of time (or any time) on Keyword Meta Tags

2. **Doing this for every page in a large site:** If you do it, just fill it in for major pages only.

3. **Using copyrighted terms:** Don't use terms that you don't own the copyright for – it's not worth being sued!

 Not used by the major search engines. Purely optional.

 This is a quick way to see what the competition is optimizing for – use "view source" in your browser and see if they've filled it in

19 Improve Page Load Speed where possible

Optional

So now you have a quality host but your pages load slowly. What's going on here?

Well, it may be that you have very image-heavy Web design, your images are not optimized for the Web, your code may be inefficient, you could have advertising that could be slowing down your page-loading or there could be other issues.

SEO value: ★★☆☆☆
Other value: ★★☆☆☆
SEO value: Page Load Speed is now a ranking factor for Google.
Other value: No one likes to go to a slow-loading page.

Google is including page load speed as a ranking factor. Also, people hate slow-loading pages. So it's in your best interest to work with your Web designer to optimize your pages to load as quickly as possible.

Resources:

These two Firefox plug-ins will help you analyze your pages and provide help and even changes to help optimize your site
- http://code.google.com/speed/page-speed/
- http://developer.yahoo.com/yslow/

Common Mistakes:

1. **Using a large background file or lots of pictures on your site:** Optimize your images and cut back on the number of images if you're overdoing it.

2. **Having your site pull information (such as advertising or widgets) from too many other sites:** Pulling data from other sites can slow down your page load speed.

 Be conscious of page load speed – it's important from a Web visitor's point of view (and Google's!)

Wrap up – 20 Essential SEO Tactics

- In this chapter we reviewed 19 SEO tactics that are essential for you to understand. You can now develop an SEO plan that includes selected "must do" and "good to do" activities.

- You can prioritize them based on your (or your company's) technical abilities, the fit with your company strategy and the potential impact to your SEO.

- Implement these tactics over time and your visibility in the search results pages should improve unless you're in a very competitive market or are targeting the wrong keywords.

- We'll cover the most important "off-page" tactic (which is really a whole strategy), Link-Building, in the following chapter.

Chapter 7. Link-Building Tactics

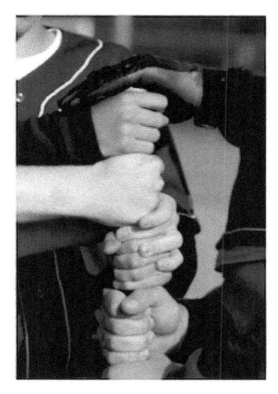

Get others to link to your Web site
to gain SEO value

Contents

A. **Link-building overview**
B. **Link-building tactics**
C. **Link-building steps**
Additional topics:
- **No follow explained**
- **PageRank Explained**

Why is Link-building important?

- For Search Engines, links (also called "hyperlinks") from pages on other people's Web sites or blogs to pages on your Web site are considered "votes" for the pages that are linked to.

- These "Inbound Links" to your pages are one of the most important factors that search engines consider when determining how important your site is.

- The search engine's view of importance of your site is the determining factor for how high up your site will show up on the Search Engine Results Page for relevant searches.

- Links from Web sites and Blog Articles are generally more important than links from Social Media Sites (LinkedIn, Facebook) and are much more important that links from comments on Blogs or in Forums.

- There are Link Quality Factors that determine the value of each Inbound Link. Some links have little to no value and others have a lot of value for SEO (see next page for more details).

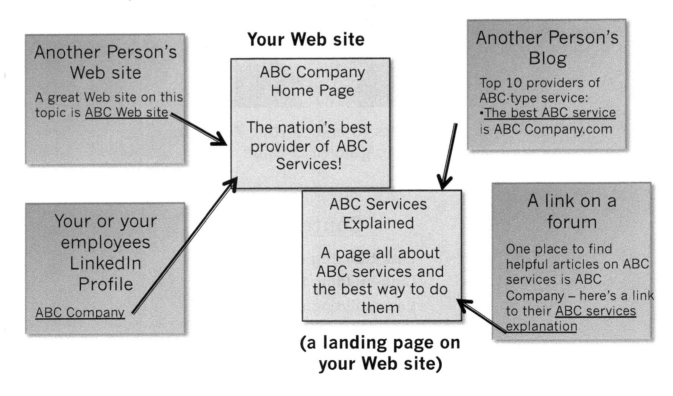

Some Link Quality Factors to consider

- **Google PageRank** of the Page – we never know the real Google PageRank of any site but can use the visible "Toolbar PageRank" as an approximation (see next page for details)

- **Location of the link** on the page – for example, there's more value to a link within the the body of an article than a link on a list of helpful resources

- **Number of outbound links** on that page – the PageRank or Link Juice given to each link is divided by the number of links on each page. The less outbound links on a page, the more each link is worth.

- **Anchor text used** – descriptive anchor text (e.g. "a great site about training dogs") is better than generic text (e.g. "click here") or your company name (e.g. "ABC Company")

- **Text surrounding the link** – the search engines can evaluate the keywords that are near the outbound link

- **Freely given link (vs. paid)** – if a link seems paid for, it will have lower value (or no value) as compared to one that seems (to the search engines) to have been freely given

- **Variety of pages** linking to your page – there is some value to having links from news sites, blogs, directories, Social Media sites versus having links coming from only one type of site

- **Variety of anchor text** – if the anchor text used for the links to your site are all the same the search engine many suspect that you're soliciting those links and devalue them. Having some variety looks more natural

- **One-way vs. reciprocal** – One way links are better than an exchange of links

- **Follow Links (vs. no-follow)** – Links that are "follow" are infinitely better for SEO than "no follow" links (but people may still click on your no follow link on a popular site so don't ignore them completely (see "No Follow Explained" for more detail).

Google PageRank Explained

Google calls its method of scoring pages PageRank (named after co-founder Larry Page). You get more PageRank (also colloquially referred to as "Link Juice" which can apply to any search engine, not just Google) passed to one of your Web pages if the page a link is coming from is a high PageRank page. Also, the less outbound links on that page, the more PageRank that is passed through each of those links. PageRank or Link Juice is basically a mechanism for search engines to measure "votes" for your page coming from other Web pages.

The catch is that you don't actually know the true PageRank of Web pages. Like many things, Google keeps this vague and ambiguous. They don't want everything spelled out because that makes it easier to game the system. But they do give you a strong clue. If you install the Google Toolbar for Internet Explorer there is a "Toolbar PageRank" that can be displayed – a green bar with a number from 0 through 10 for any page (if you hover hover your cursor over the small bar). Also, there are many other tools, including Firefox plugins that will show Toolbar PageRank. Toolbar PageRank gives you a directional indicator of a web page's PageRank although some think it's very inaccurate and out of date.

At the end of the day, the true PageRank of any given page is not perfectly clear but, that doesn't mean you should completely discount Toolbar PageRank. Clearly some indication is better than none, so high "Toolbar PageRank" sites should be targeted in your link-building efforts. If you plan on asking for a link or would like to write a guest post on another site, you should aim for higher quality sites and Toolbar PageRank is one of the criteria to select the target sites. Also, your own page's Toolbar PageRank increases can be seen as a rough indicator of growing authority in Google's eyes.

The Wall Street Journal's home page has a Toolbar PageRank of 8 out of 10

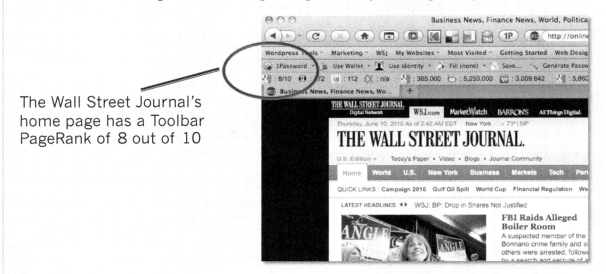

No Follow Explained

- Search engines have methods of valuing links from one site to another. This helps them automatically determine which pages are more authoritative when a search is run. But there are times when you want to put up a link to another site or allow people to place links on your site but you don't want to reward them by passing some of your web page's PageRank (or link juice). Here are some examples:

  - You may sell advertising on your site with a link to another site. You don't want to run afoul of Google's policy of not passing PageRank for purchased links.

  - You might have a link to a site that you don't like. You want to have the link but not pass any valuable "link juice" to them.

  - You might want people respond to your blog posts with new, helpful information, valid questions or even with links to related articles or tools. But if each responder gets "link juice" by putting a link underneath your blog post, there will be a great incentive for people to put spam on your blog linking to their Viagra or porn sites or other unrelated Web sites.

  - For Social Media sites much of their content is user-generated content, These sites want to reduce the incentive for people to put links up purely to get "link juice" coming back to their own sites

- So because Google, Yahoo! And Bing all want you to be able to do these things without passing "link juice", they created the "nofollow" tag which Webmasters can put on their Web pages next to links that they don't want the search engines passing Link Juice to.

- No Follow is often built into a Content Management (for blog comments), Blogging Systems (comments), Social Media sites (most areas where you can put links) and Forums (usually these are No Follow) or can be added by a Webmaster. These sites want to decrease the benefits of putting spammy links on their pages. People still put their links to Viagra or porn sites but it would probably be worse if they were rewarded with Link Juice!

- Some of the various Firefox SEO plugins or other tools check for no follow tags on the Web page you're visiting.

What are different ways to build links? Here are some different ways…

1. Be Linked To – People decide that your site, page or article is worth linking to

2. Ask - Ask for a Link – "will you put a link to my site on your site?" This works well if it's a close partner, a site with some of your competitors listed or is a friend. Don't forget to ask for good anchor text for the link.

3. Submit - Submit a Link to a site or directory that accepts links

4. Exchange - Ask to trade links with someone or join a Link Exchange program. These are not as good as one-way links.

5. Pay for a Link – Buy a link or an ad with a link on someone's site. Just be careful about running afoul of Google's terms of service by getting caught buying obviously purchased links.

6. Article or Guest Blog Post - Write an article or blog post with links to your site that you or someone else puts up on a site or blog

7. Comment - Write a comment at the bottom of someone's Blog Post or in an Online Forum that includes a link to your site (usually a "no follow" link)

8. Social Media Links - Put a link in a Social Media site in a profile section or other area (usually a "no follow" link)

9. Review Sites – You, someone else or a listing is created for your Web site on an online review Web site.

10. Directories or Internet Yellow Pages (IYP) – You create or a listing is created for your business that links to your Web site.

11. Local Sites – Local directories like CitySearch that include links to your site.

12. Google Places/Bing Local - You create a listing on a search engine local site that includes a link to your Web site.

13. Organizations/Associations - Membership in industry or local organizations or associations that include links.

14. Your Sites/Blogs- Links from other sites you manage.

15. Get a link on the Open Directory (www.DMOZ.org). It's a high value link for SEO that's free but it can take a long time to actually get a link and you may never get one. The site is run by volunteers.

16. Pay for a link at a respected directory. The Yahoo Directory or the Best of the Web directory are considered high value paid directories.

What is the best method of building links?

Hands down, the best way to get links is **"Be Linked To"** due to the **great information** you have on your site (your "Killer Content"). This means that people see your site, page, article or video as valuable for their audience, friends, customers and readers, they link to you. But for people to find your information, it needs to be promoted.

Why is getting people to link to your site via good content a good thing?

- **The links will come organically** – you don't need to spend extra effort to ask for them, pay for them or submit them

- **The links will not look like they are asked for, paid for or part of a link exchange program** because there will be a variety of sites linking, they will use different anchor text and they will build up over time (versus come all at once)

- You have **a higher chance of getting better quality sites** to link to you – asking for links from good sites will usually not get you far

What are the challenges?

- **Your content has to be better** than most content that exists for your industry. If you're the only plumber in town that has quality blog posts, how-to articles or video, you'll probably get links to your site!

- **You need to promote your great content** in as many ways as possible – newsletters, blog posts, PR, letting related bloggers and influencers know, and especially via Social Media

- **You may have many "misses" before you have a "hit"**. Don't give up too quickly

 Have such <u>great content</u> that people link to you from their Web sites or Blogs

Blogging Attracts More Links

Blogging is often the best place to get lots of quality content on your site. That's why companies that actively blog get more inbound links pointing to them.

As you can see below, according to a survey by the company Hubspot, companies that blog have about double the inbound links that an companies that don't.

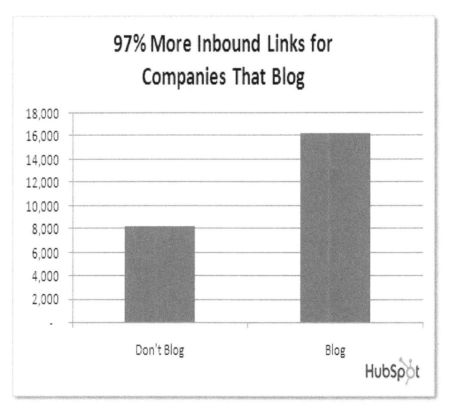

Source: Data from over 1,500 small businesses · http://bit.ly/XDkQV

Wrap-Up: Link-building steps

Now that you understand the importance of link-building and some of the key ways to can get links, here is a simple process you can follow. Customize it as needed for your business and resources available

Evaluate progress and repeat as needed

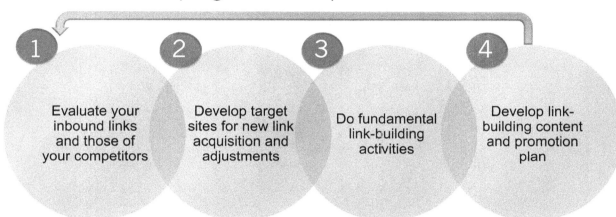

1 — Evaluate your inbound links and those of your competitors	2 — Develop target sites for new link acquisition and adjustments	3 — Do fundamental link-building activities	4 — Develop link-building content and promotion plan
•Measure your current links in terms of number and quality using link-checking tools mentioned in chapter 5 •Evaluate top offline and online competitors' backlinks •Look for backlink opportunities and issues with your current backlinks	•Identify top industry sites, blogs and directories for backlinks •Combine with backlinks identified from competitor research •Begin to establish relationships with key industry bloggers, news sites or associations. Reach out to them or make insightful comments on their blogs as a way to connect.	•Do the basic link-building – e.g. directory submissions, internet yellow page submissions, link requests, paid memberships and requests to improve current inbound inks •Submit site to Social Media sites and link from company and employee profiles	•Develop "linkable" content development strategy •Tie link-building and content development strategies to Social Media as well as additional offline/ online promotion strategies •Focus on getting your content noticed by key industry bloggers, journals and influencers •Submit killer content to industry news sites, associations or blogs that may want to feature your content or point it out to their audience or members

Chapter 8. "Killer" Content Creation for SEO Value

What content will draw in your audience, teach them something valuable and compel them to share with others?

Contents

A. **Content creation overview**

B. **Web site content**

C. **Blog content**

D. **Educational content**

Additional:

- **Benefits of Regular Blogging**
- **Killer Content Ideas**

Why is content so important?

- **It contributes significantly to better SEO**
  - It can attract quality links if your content is great and is effectively promoted
  - Content is like food for the search engine spiders. More content provides you with more opportunity to emphasize target keywords (and other long-tail keywords) with the search engines

- **It helps with Conversions**
  - Content engages and educates visitors
  - Keeps them on your site longer and keeps them coming back
  - Earns trust
  - Can incent visitors to provide you with their information in exchange for something (e.g. white paper, tutorial, etc.)

- **It can encourage promotion via Social Media**
  - If set up properly for sharing, blogs, articles or video can easily be shared and re-shared with your contacts' networks

The big three content areas to focus on at first

Focus your initial content development on three areas:

1. Web site Content: Creating engaging and keyword-rich content for your Web site

2. Blog: compelling and keyword-rich content; this will lead to more sharing and potentially inbound linking to your blog posts

3. Educational Content: Finding a unique (for your industry) angle to really educate your potential customers and influencers and mouthpieces in the industry; can be part of your blog or Web site and can also be posted outside of your Web site

- About your company
- Your products/services and their descriptions
- Your location and how to contact you
- Company-related videos, pictures, press releases
- Landing pages and conversion actions

1) Your Web site Content

2) Your Blog Content

3) Your Educational Content

- Information about the company
- Perspective on industry news
- Reviews
- Announcements
- Opinion
- Fun articles
- Videos
- Articles by guest writers
- Educational articles

- Videos
- Articles
- White papers
- Glossaries
- Infographics
- Information and links about useful resources

Other content to think about after focusing on the three above...

User-generated content

Any other content you can imagine or find online

Content you produce and post outside of your Web site

1) Optimize and Expand Your main Web site Content

Must Do!*

Your main Web site content refers to the basic pages and information you require on your site. These are most likely to be fairly static so make it as good and SEO-friendly as possible the first time around. Also, build good SEO practices into your Web design and update processes so it become part of the program. Here are tips to making your Web site content as effective as possible for SEO.

1. Write more (quality) content than you may be comfortable with – shoot to have between 200-400 words/page if possible

2. Follow the SEO rules from Chapter 6 for all of your main pages

   • Keyword phrases in page titles

   • One H1 tag per page (if possible) including target keyword phrase; keywords in the headers where practical

   • Use bold or strong with keywords

   • Include picture alt tags and captions

   • Write video descriptions or include text from the transcripts of the videos

   • Within the content, include links to other related content on your site (with anchor text) and to outbound (but non-competitive) authority sites as appropriate

3. Don't use the exactly the same content as other Web sites

   • Change file names and descriptions for media that you get from elsewhere (pictures, video)

   • Make product descriptions unique – not the same as other Web sites selling that product

4. Use a variety of media – lots of HTML text but also include video and pictures

5. Educate your audience – create "how to's" or other informational articles or videos

6. You can make it interesting or entertaining - don't think you have to write dry, boring content

7. For any articles or educational content, make it easy to share via Social Media – use share buttons on these pages

8. It shouldn't stay completely static. Review and update your main Web site content periodically

9. Use good copywriting for your site – don't give it to the intern. Make sure your best writers work on this

10. Don't forget about your conversion goals – design key pages for the actions you desire

11. Appearance is important. The same content on an ugly Web site is not as effective as it will be on a nice Web site with a reasonable amount of graphics and pictures

---

Common Mistakes:

1. **Delegating Web site content to less capable writers:** Your Web site content doesn't change much, is a key part of your SEO and is what customers see every time they come to your site. Take the time to make it excellent.

2. **Being skimpy with words:** If you're a person of few words, you need to break that habit when it comes to Web copywriting.

3. **Ignoring the SEO basics from Chapter 6:** Keep a copy of this chapter available when you're writing content for your site.

 Your main Web site content is more static than your blog. Take the time to develop plenty of good content that stands the test of time and that helps your SEO by using the target keyword phrases.

2) Develop an effective Blog Strategy

Must Do!*

Your blog is an extension of your site. It's an opportunity to add content to your site quickly in a less organized fashion. It can be more spontaneous, more casual and occasionally off-topic. It can be a release valve for content that you'd like to get out but that normally would require a Web site redesign or addition of a new page to fit in. Blog posts also contribute to SEO by adding content, keyword phrases. Here are guidelines for blogging effectively.

1. Make sure your blog is set up under your domain so your site gets any SEO value you create

2. Start out by picking a general theme and writing style for your blog – you can evolve this over time but it helps to know what you're trying to accomplish and the type of content and tone of your blog

3. Create an editorial calendar of planned posts or topic with a timeline. You can mix in spontaneous posts as you go.

4. Put someone in charge of making sure the content gets created and posted (and is good!)

5. Make sure the content is easy to share. Blog posts are particularly common to share due to the very topical, educational, interesting or humorous nature. You need to have Social Media share buttons on your blog posts

6. Don't make the content too dry!

7. Mix up the topics, style or medium on occasion. Keep people interested

8. Decide on a frequency and try to stick to it – don't over commit yourself

9. Encourage audience interaction and engage with commenters

10. Go outside your blog – make value-added comments on related or industry blogs – you can leave your blog's URL or reference a related post but don't spam or overtly advertise without giving quality comments

11. Consider integrating guest posts or user-generated content into some of your posts

12. Be creative in terms of the blog post topics or format:

- Interview an industry expert
- Do an ongoing series on a hot topic
- Do video instead of a text post to mix it up
- Show another side of your company
- Create education articles or how-to's
- Do something humorous

13. Personalize it

- Let down your guard a little
- Show your company in the community
- Introduce key members of your staff
- Allow staff or partners to write an article to show their expertise or to comment on industry trends

---

Common Mistakes:

1. **Making excuses to not start Blogging:** In the beginning you are writing for an audience of very few. Don't forget though that this content helps your SEO. You'll also get good practice in writing effective blog posts – this will serve you well when you have more readers.

2. **Being boring and dry on your blog:** Make it fun, interesting or informative but not boring.

3. **Over-committing and not following through:** Set an internal goal for your blog frequency and see how this works for your company. Adjust as needed but don't give up on blogging.

4. **Forgetting the SEO Basics** for each Blog post including keyword-rich page titles, headers, content and picture alt tag (see all of the basics in chapter 6).

 Each blog post (especially if it's a really good one) can pay dividends for years by helping you get found via search engines or links. Take the time to plan and write (or film or record) great content!

Degrees of Blogging

You get more benefits the more time and energy you put into your Blog. But there are benefits to even an infrequent blog (from the additional content and keywords).

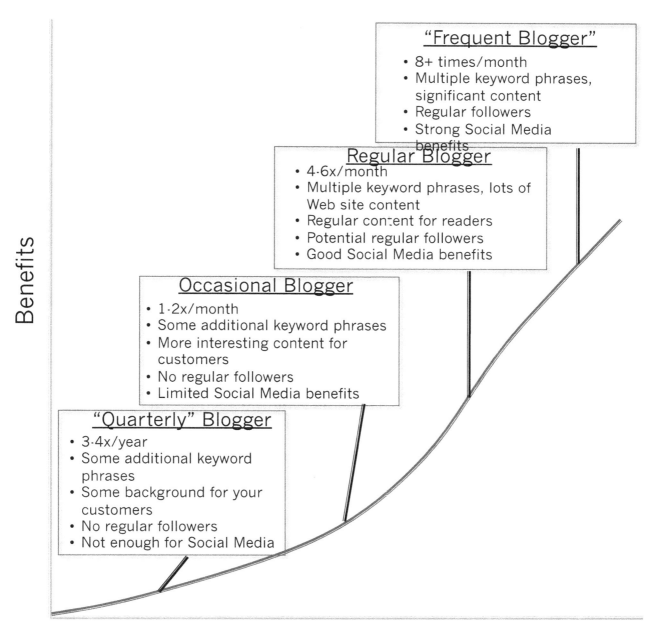

"Frequent Blogger"
- 8+ times/month
- Multiple keyword phrases, significant content
- Regular followers
- Strong Social Media benefits

Regular Blogger
- 4-6x/month
- Multiple keyword phrases, lots of Web site content
- Regular content for readers
- Potential regular followers
- Good Social Media benefits

Occasional Blogger
- 1-2x/month
- Some additional keyword phrases
- More interesting content for customers
- No regular followers
- Limited Social Media benefits

"Quarterly" Blogger
- 3-4x/year
- Some additional keyword phrases
- Some background for your customers
- No regular followers
- Not enough for Social Media

Benefits (y-axis)

Investment in Time, Energy (x-axis)

*Data has shown that companies that blog more acquire more customers through their Web sites

What are the benefits of blogging regularly?

* The search engines will crawl sites more often if they are regularly updated

* Blogging allows you to add keyword rich content to your site, reinforcing relevancy with the search engines

* Writing blog posts allows you to use various forms of your keywords and additional phrases you may not have used in your main Web site. These can help you catch searches for long-tail and local keywords

* Blogging lets your company have a less formal communication vehicle with customers and lets them get to know you and your company (leading to more comfort and trust)

* People share and link to blog posts that they find useful or interesting

* You can connect your blog posts to your Social Media sites so when you have new blog posts they can manually or automatically share via Facebook, LinkedIn, Twitter and others.

 Blogging is a great way to quickly and easily add SEO-friendly content to your Web site

Must
Do!

3) Well-placed Educational Content

A major reason people go online is to find educational material. I don't mean "school" per se. I mean how-to articles, best practices, videos explaining how things work, how to fix something, how to buy something, how to "do-it-yourself", checklists and more. They also are looking for education on which products and services will work best for them, how to choose, and what an appropriate price might be.

Search engines also love Web pages that contain how-to or reference materials. If your company develops great educational material you'll have a leg up on your competition in terms of getting more links, having better SEO and generally satisfying your potential customers more.

Tips for your Educational Content:

1. Think from a customer's perspective. What information would be most valuable to them? What content will differentiate your educational content from the competition? For example, if your competitors have a "how-to" article on installing hardwood flooring, how about one-upping them with a video?

2. Ask your customers what "how-to" or reference materials would be most valuable to them? Ask your salespeople what types of questions the customers typically ask.

3. If you post your content on an external site, make sure you also have some different version of it on your site so you get the SEO value coming to your site as well.

    • YouTube Video – if you post a video on YouTube, post a version directly on your site as well. Or you can also post a transcript of the video to also get SEO value from text.

    • If you post an article on another site – post some similar information on your site as well but make sure you change it enough that Google won't see it as identical content.

4. Make your great educational content "share-able" in Social Media sites by using share buttons and encouraging or asking people to share.

5.   Like a movie studio, you may have some "misses" before you have a "hit". Keep at it, listen to feedback and let your company improve in its content creation through practice.

6.   Promote your great content via Social Media – for example post the description and a link to Twitter, Facebook, LinkedIn and Plaxo.

7.   Get creative with your educational content ideas. Don't be too conservative!

8.   In addition to educational content that goes on your Web site, you can leverage your great content ideas to do Webinars, include them in newsletters and to develop courses or eBooks.

Common Mistakes:

1.   **Thinking you don't have anything to teach:** Don't assume your potential customers all know the basics of your industry, products and services. Start simple and lay out the basics.

2.   **Being afraid to share too much information:** The benefits of attracting more customers, getting better search engine rankings and gaining the respect and trust of your potential customers usually outweigh negatives from sharing some of your proprietary information.

3.   **Doing nothing:** If you want to gain access to more potential customers (whether you're looking for individual customers or large corporate customers), you should be creating educational content that will help them.

 Educational content, including videos, articles, email newsletters with industry information, training courses, webinars and more are key lures for potential customers and can help with SEO as well.

Before you decide on the content to create, ask yourself a few questions

Before you develop major content pieces (articles, video, how-to guides, white papers, eBooks) for your Web site or Blog, here are some questions you can ask yourself to help you determine the right content and promotion strategy:

- What kind of content is out there already? What are the competitors doing?

- What are some gaps or new ideas for content?

- Will this be useful or interesting to our end users and customers?

- Who are the types of people that might link to us (top bloggers, site owners, industry periodicals, etc.)?

- What's the best way to reach the key bloggers, site owners or industry periodicals?

- What's in it for them? Why would these industry people link to you? To get a scoop? To provide a useful tool or a bit of entertainment for their audience?

 Think about your audience, your goals and, very importantly, your promotion strategy for your content. Who can help your content be found by the right audience?

Ideas for Killer Content

- User-generated content – have a contest where people shoot pictures or video using your product! Post the best ones and crown a winner!

- Create a unique "Infographic" that pictorially explains a key concept or that shows data in a unique way

- Create an industry-wide useful resource such as a glossary of industry terms that people can send their customers to.

- Do a how-to video or article about how to build something, use something, buy something, etc.

- Do a checklist (e.g. top 10 reasons to remodel your bathroom)

- Run a regular article or video series on trends in your industry

- Do a regular video course on essential topics in your industry (e.g. Woodworking 101)

- Post great photos of recent projects you've completed (so your customers can link to it or email it to their friends and family)

- Do a Q&A forum related to your industry where people write in questions and you answer them online (text or video)

- Do a survey of customers or people in the industry and post the key findings

- Do an in-depth interview of an industry guru

- A periodic light-hearted (morning radio show-type) show to discuss trends in your industry

- Guest posts written by industry luminaries or your company's partners

"Pull "is always better than "Push" – if you can create content that compels people to link to your site (pull) it's so much better and less time-intensive than requesting, buying or submitting for links (push).

Some thoughts before you dive into your Killer Content strategy development

- You need to learn how to be a "content publisher" for the purposes of SEO and increased customer engagement

- Content publishing is like being in the movie industry – you'll need to make a few losers before you have a hit!

- You'll get better over time and will learn from the feedback and interaction with customers and people in your industry

- Some things won't be a hit at first but will build slowly (so don't give up on them)

- Promotion (next step) is a critical part of the whole process

- Just go for it! You have a lot more to win than you have to lose

 Don't be impatient with your content strategy. You'll usually have more losers than winners but keep at it!

Chapter 9. Using Social Media for promotion of your content

Spread the news via Social Media applications
like Facebook, Twitter and LinkedIn

Contents

A. **Overview of Social Media**
B. **Social Media promotion steps**
C. **Social Media platforms and tools**
Additional:
  ▪ **Social Review Sites List**
  ▪ **Social Media Management Tools**

You need to promote your "Killer Content"

Killer content is the best way to attract people to link to your site. If you get high quality links, that's great for SEO and also you'll get additional traffic when people see those links and click on them. So, if you have "killer", or even just "good", content, what are the best ways to get people to see it and then possibly link to you?

- Just like a product, you have to promote it! What are the ways to promote it?

- Advertise it – you can do a pay per click campaign on Google (pay people to check out your content)

- Tell your list – if you have a mailing list, you can email it to them

- Word of mouth – you can tell people you know about your content

- Via your RSS feed – people can subscribe to the "RSS feed" of your blog. This means people will receive a copy of your content via email or on an RSS reader every time you create a new blog post

- Social Media – you can promote it through Facebook, Twitter, LinkedIn, Flickr, YouTube and more

- Most importantly – Find the information-gatherers in your industry (top blogs, industry trade associations, online journals, news Web sites or others) and make them aware of your content

- You can also talk with industry blogs or sites about guest-posting a blog article on their site.

In this section we'll be talking about promoting your Web site content via Social Media platforms such as Twitter, LinkedIn and Facebook. Social Media is uniquely suited to promoting content online, is very complementary to your SEO efforts and has the potential to spread your content farther and faster than any other vehicle. We'll explain why on the following pages.

 For content: "If you build it…they won't come". You need to promote it in as scalable a way as possible

What sites are considered Social Media?

- Social Networking
  - Facebook, MySpace
- Business Social Networking
  - LinkedIn. Plaxo
- Photo Sharing
  - Flickr, Picasa, Photobucket
- Video Sharing
  - YouTube, Vimeo
- Social Reviewing
  - Yelp, Kudzu, Angie's List, Epinions
- Microblogging
  - Twitter, Yammer
- Social Bookmarking/Social News
  - Delicious, StumbleUpon, Digg

 There are a lot of Social Media sites out there but often you can connect them together so your information gets posted across multiple sites when you're ready to share

So who's using Social Media?

Across all demographics the usage of Social Media applications is growing rapidly. As an example of the tremendous growth, in July of 2010 Facebook hit its 500 millionth user worldwide.

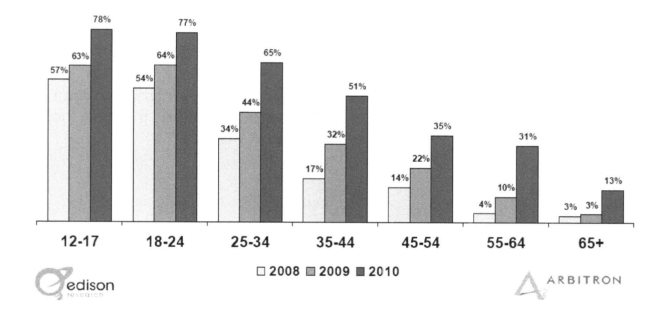

% by Age Group Who Currently Have a Personal Profile Page on Facebook, MySpace, LinkedIn or Any Other Social Networking Web Site

□ 2008 ▨ 2009 ■ 2010

edison

ARBITRON

The people who can provide links to your site (based on your content) are using Social Media. So are many of your customers!

Why do people get involved in Social Media?

- **Desire to Connect** with their friends and coworkers
- **Desire to Participate** and be involved where their friends are
- **Desire to Learn** (by finding information, tips, resources online)
- **Desire to be Entertained** – some people want to find entertaining content via Social Media
- **Desire to Grow their Network** – Some people want a broader reach that more connections provides them
- **Desire for Status** – Sharing great content can give you higher status in the Social Media world
- **Desire to Share** – Some people want to share information about themselves or great content they created or found; this can include entertaining content such as a YouTube video

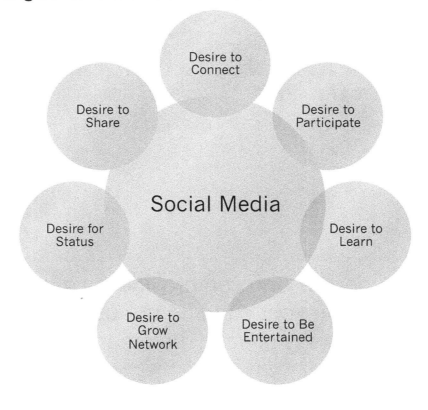

In Social Media, Content is the "Fuel" that keeps the machine running

Once you're connected to people via a Social Media platform, the only way you connect again, reach out or stand out is via the creation of or sharing of content. Whether it is a simple status post, a site you like, a great restaurant you found, a picture of the family, a blog post you wrote or great information you found and want to pass on.

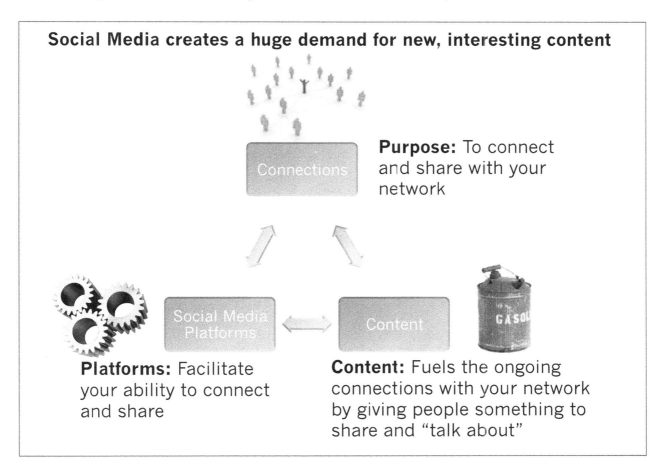

Social Media creates a huge demand for new, interesting content

Connections

Purpose: To connect and share with your network

Social Media Platforms

Content

Platforms: Facilitate your ability to connect and share

Content: Fuels the ongoing connections with your network by giving people something to share and "talk about"

Content is the fuel of Social Media. Because of this there is a voracious appetite for new and interesting content. If you have the right content for your audience this can be one of your best promotional vehicles

Social Media makes it very easy to connect with others and to share all kinds of Content

- Easily share interesting blog posts, articles, pictures or videos that you find right from the content directly to your Twitter, Facebook, or Delicious profile

- Easily post videos, pictures or links to your profile for sharing

- "Like", "ReTweet" or repost comments or information you want to share with your network

- Connect once with each contact and then your contacts are always "opted in" to your updates

- Your networks connect to the networks of each of your contacts allowing you content to spread broadly

- You can easily publish new blog content simultaneously on multiple Social Media sites

- Joining groups in Facebook and LinkedIn allows you to connect with your target demographic and engage with them

- Tools such as Linkedin Discussion and Yahoo! Answers make it easy to answer other people's questions where you can display your expertise to a broad set of people

Example of sharing buttons at the bottom of a Blog post:

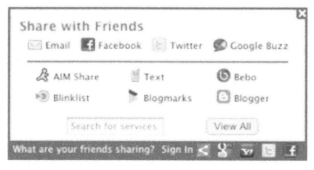

 Social Media easily facilitates connecting with others (including your target demographic) and sharing content

Going Viral: How content can spread via Social Media

Your social network connecting to their social networks

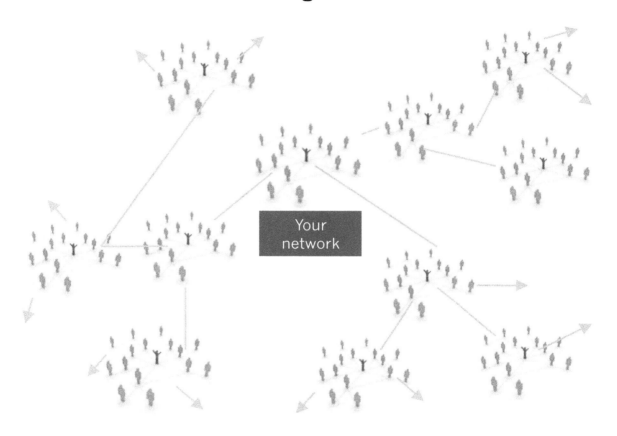

Great Content can "Go Viral" when it's "liked" and shared across networks and even across Social Media platforms

 Social Media can help great information spread quickly from network to network

Why is Social Media better in many cases than email?

Advantages of Social Media vs. Email:

- Once you connect with someone, they can view all of your shared content as you publish it

- If people like your content, they can "like", share or repost it, spreading it to their contacts and potentially those contacts' networks

- There are no emails to delete for the receiver. It's like a constant stream of information they can review or interact with as they see fit with no clean up needed

- You can connect your blog and Social Media sites so that all of your blog posts are automatically broadcast to your connections

- No formatting of email newsletters, list management and issues with being seen as a spammer

- People can share to their Social Media applications directly from interesting articles, blog posts or videos so they don't have to deal with copying links and opening their application separately

 With Social Media, people only have to opt-in once (i.e. accept your connection invitation) and then they will be constantly connected to anything you share with them!

Learn what makes content "share-worthy"

- Social Media is designed as a vehicle to post, share and re-share content with people in your network. If there's no content, there's very little interaction in Social Media.

- Articles, videos, pictures, reviews, comments (and more) are the fuel of Social Media. They're like the gas in the car or the wood in the fire. It's a requirement.

- Take a look at a Facebook page, a Twitter Feed or the bottom of a LinkedIn page. You should notice a lot of content being shared. People share what they find interesting, useful, entertaining or educational.

- Take a little time each week and click on some of the things people are sharing. What makes these things "share-worthy"? The better you understand this, the easier it will be to apply it to your content creation and Social Media promotion activities.

 To successfully promote your content, think about the types of people that share content and what would motivate them to share yours

 While you target potential customers with your content, for link-building you target bloggers and Web site owners

Why do blogging and Social Media fit so well together?

- **Your great content usually starts at your blog:** Your blog is typically the place where you'll put your interesting and up-to-date content. Your great article, your "top 10 tips" post, your "how to" video, your white paper, your photography shoot photos…

- **Blog posts are usually "bite-sized":** Your blog posts are not usually long essay. They're usually articles that can be read or viewed in 2-3 minutes.

- **Blog posts are often topical or timely:** More often blog posts are timely or focused on a very specific topic as opposed to your Web site content which is timeless and more general.

- **Blogs and Social Media sites are easy to integrate:** You can set it up so your blog posts are automatically shared on your Twitter, Facebook or LinkedIn accounts (as well as other social networks) or you can just post the links and a description manually. This can get them noticed.

- **Blogs often include easy Social Media share mechanisms:** Look at your favorite blogs. If you see buttons that say things like "Share This" or if you see the Facebook, Twitter or other icons near each post, these are meant for people to easily share via their Social Media profiles.

 Blogs and Social Media go hand-in-hand. Blogs are the content repositories. Social Media sites are the promotion vehicles.

Promoting via Social Media – Key Steps

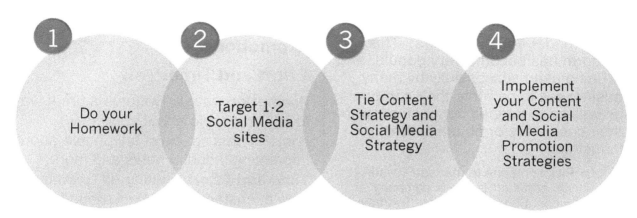

1 Do your Homework

- Where do your customers congregate?
- What are your competitors doing?
- Set up individual accounts to learn the ropes of potential Social Media vehicles
- Make connections and observe how other companies are using the sites to promote their content
- Identify the key "information hubs" (blogs, news sites, industry associations) in your industry or geographic area

2 Target 1-2 Social Media sites

- Determine which sites fit best into your strategy - pick 1-2 platforms
- Learn the best practices for these platforms
- Pick a lead to manage each effort
- Determine what tools can help you manage or automate your Social Media activities

3 Tie Content Strategy and Social Media Strategy

- Determine which content you'll be developing over time
- Develop a sharing, commenting and response strategy for your Social Media platforms
- Promote your blog posts, specials and other company highlights (if appropriate) via Social Media
- Make sure the industry or local "information hubs" are aware of your relevant content

4 Implement your Content and Social Media Promotion Strategies

- Launch Social Media profiles for your company
- Comment, share, respond and post your company's content and interesting and relevant industry information
- Develop a following
- Highlight your "link-worthy" content on your own site and encourage sharing and re-posting
- Submit links for you content to key industry blogs, news sites or others who are in a position to share it broadly (but be sensitive to their requirements)

 Like most other things, go slow with your Social Media efforts. Keep your eyes open and watch how others use it to engage with their audience and to subtly promote their brand.

Promotion Via Twitter

Good to Do!

Twitter is a platform that allows your company to create and share short posts (under 140 characters). This platform has become very popular and is being used successfully by many businesses to promote their companies as well as to deepen connections with their customers or others in their industries.

- Pick someone to manage Twitter – you can start with one company account but some companies have multiple accounts for different people or divisions

- Determine a content generation strategy – in addition to sharing great content from your site (e.g. a highlight and a link), you need to determine what type of information you'll be Tweeting and how often (roughly)

Promotion value: ★★★★☆

Effort and Time: *Low*

Promotion value: Twitter is a great way to inform people about your new content, post specials, tell people about interesting industry news and more.

Time and Effort: Setting up a Twitter profile, customizing a background and getting the word out to contacts, friends and customers is fairly easy. Also, by using automated tools such as Hootsuite you can spend an hour each Monday and have your Tweets scheduled to post throughout the week.

- Determine a content sharing strategy – what sources will you look at and what types of info will you retweet or share (from others). For example go to www.alltop.com to see the top blogs for almost any industry or topic.

- Get your blog feed connected to Twitter so that each blog post automatically generates a link on Twitter

- To make it easier you can use a platform like HootSuite to schedule Tweets (you can prepare several Tweets on Monday and spread them out throughout the week)

People follow people or companies they like and will look at or "retweet" great content. People are also doing searches in Twitter on various topics so your content can be discovered that way. Lastly the search engines are starting to pick up Twitter posts for their search results so more and more Tweets will be found online based on people's searches.

Fairly easy to set-up and manage, Twitter can be an effective promotion tool for your content, company happenings, industry news and specials.

Content Promotion via a Facebook page

While people have personal profiles in Facebook, companies have pages called "Company Pages". Facebook frowns upon using a personal page for a business and may delete your account. You can use the approach below to develop a Facebook strategy:

Promotion value: ★★★★☆

Effort and Time: *Medium to High*

Promotion value: Facebook is one of the best ways to promote your company and your great content.
Time and Effort: Expectations are higher for Facebook in terms of number of posts, quality of content and set-up of a Facebook page. Be prepared to invest time and effort but the payoffs can be great.

- Via your personal Facebook profile, join some company pages to see how other companies are using their Facebook Pages to have a conversation with their audience and generate interest in their companies

- When you're ready, create a Facebook Page for your company. Customize it to include information about your company, the purpose of the page, your logo and other design elements.

- Hook up your blog posts (and YouTube, Twitter) to feed into the Facebook page. Additionally, you'll want to create posts directly into Facebook to get get conversations going. You can ask questions, run contests, advertise webinars and more.

- Get your employees and customers to join – advertise the ability to join you in Facebook on your Web site, in your email footers, at conferences and in other marketing materials.

- To be valuable you need to keep up some activity in Facebook, so be prepared with a plan to generate posts and to respond to your member's questions or posts – you should have someone assigned to manage the page

- Some creative ways to use Facebook include:

  - A translation business that sends out a "word of the day" post for foreign languages (hits on everyone's interest to learn and keeps that firm top of mind)

  - A marketing firm that sends out "how to" posts on a regular basis (how can you not read a "how to article!")

  - A photographer that includes a couple of great pictures from each photo shoot (very shareable!)

 You need to make your Facebook posts and content interesting, informative, fun and/or engaging – not dry product announcements only!

Content promotion with YouTube

YouTube allows you to post videos and to even create a company channel. This is a great way to get people on YouTube finding your content.

> **Promotion value:** ★★★☆☆
>
> **Effort and Time:** *Medium to High*
>
> **Promotion value**: Getting your great videos onto YouTube is an excellent way to promote your company.
>
> **Time and Effort:** If you already have videos, you should post them both to your site and YouTube (create a channel) – this is easy. Developing the video content is the most time-consuming part.

- Make sure you do the following:

  - Optimize your content as much as possible with the right keywords

- You can create a video version of a good blog post or article you've posted on your site

- Make sure your site's URL and any relevant contact information is clearly highlighted on your channel, early in each video's description and in the video itself

- You can post a YouTube version of a video in YouTube but you can post the original directly on your site (without YouTube) so you have two chances of your video being found

- Share your videos in Facebook, Twitter and on your Web site!

 Some people respond much better to Video than to the written word. Create your first video and utilize your Web site, YouTube and your other Social Media sites to promote it!

Optional

Content promotion via Flickr (or Picasa and Photobucket)

Flickr is a photo-sharing site. Businesses are discouraged from explicitly advertising on Flickr but there are ways to post your content and get some potential traffic and attention via Flckr.

Promotion value: ★★☆☆☆

Effort and Time: *Low*

Promotion value: If there is a pictorial or graphical element to your business, getting keyword-rich photo content in Flickr can be a great way to be found. **Time and Effort:** Actively posting the pictures, getting the titles and descriptions in and making sure they're linked to your blog adds some extra time but can be worth it.

- Create an account with your business URL as your name so people can find your site

- Make sure your pictures have descriptive titles and that the descriptions include keywords and your URL

- You can use the Flickr page to host pictures that are on your blog posts. Rather than loading the pictures into your blog you can link to them from your posts.

- Each time you create a post your descriptive pictures can be added to your Flickr site – this builds up a wealth of keyword-rich pictures

- You can join Flickr groups related to your business to get more exposure with people who are interested in that topic.

- People searching in Flickr or in the search engines will have the opportunity to discover your pictures which can lead them to your site

 Use Flickr (or similar sites), especially if your business has a photographic or graphical element to it

LinkedIn (or Plaxo)

LinkedIn is the top business social networking site. It's also a profitable company so it is definitely doing something right! LinkedIn has several great ways to get the word out about your company and your great content:

Promotion value: ★★★☆☆
Effort and Time: *Low*

Promotion value: LinkedIn can lead to getting your business noticed by people in your industry or even potential customers.

Time and Effort: Using LinkedIn to promote your Web site and content and to show your company's expertise (by answering questions) can be fairly minimal. Starting and managing a group can take more thought and effort.

- Make sure your employee's profiles includes links to your Web site (in the My Web sites section) and you can also link to key new products or landing pages you want to promote.

- Ask a question – You can ask a question viewable by all of your contacts that can get your name out their or lead to engagement – it can be a question like, "does anyone have advice on the best way to market affordable strategy consulting services to medium businesses in the East Coast?"

- Answer a question – People ask questions like: How do I assess a Web site hosting company? If you're in a related business you can show your expertise by answering a question – they may just check out your profile or Web site

- Join Groups – when you join a group, certain activities you do (such as ask a question, answer a question, promote your content) will be sent to all members

- Start a group – If you want to get people who are interested in a certain topic you can start a group and advertise it – you can have potential customers join your group if it sounds like it will put them together with like minded people who can help them out

 People often overlook the many various sharing and connecting options available in LinkedIn

Social Review Sites:
Yelp, Kudzu or Angie's List

For the cities where Yelp is active, it can be a big generator of traffic for local businesses. You may not have a choice on whether or not to be on Yelp – if someone submits your company, you're in! Also, you have to have thick skin – you may get negative reviews.

There are also a lot of other Social Review sites including Kudzu, Angie's List and more (see next page for a list).

Promotion value: ⭐⭐⭐⭐⭐

Effort and Time: *Low*

Promotion value: Review sites can generate a lot of traffic – especially for local businesses.

Time and Effort: Owning (or creating) your company profile is fairly easy. It takes some time to make sure it has content-rich keywords, pictures, descriptions of your products/services, store hours, etc. Also, dealing with negative reviews can take time (don't fight online!) and be distracting.

- If your site is there, make sure you take control of it and put in pictures, a good description, other key information and your Web site URL

- If you get negative reviews that are extremely harsh or unfair, use the tools, if needed, to address it with the poster or respond online but don't escalate it into a fight.

- Encourage people to review you in Yelp but don't go overboard – Yelp's system may cull out reviews if they think you're actively soliciting reviews or if they're all "too good"

 Yelp can be a great traffic generator but local businesses sometimes feel frustrated when they receive what seems like unfair or harsh criticism

Review Frenzy: The many faces of Social Review Sites

There are a lot of Social Review sites out there. If you're game to get exposure for your business and can take some negative reviews as well, get your business in these sites:

- Yelp!
- Rate it All
- Kudzu.com
- Angie's List
- Merchant Circle
- Yellow Bot
- Brown Book
- Service Magic
- Judy's Book
- Praized
- City Voter
- Insider Pages

Actively participating in Social Bookmarking and Social News sites

Optional

Social Bookmarking sites like Delicious, Digg, Mixx, Linkvine and more are designed to allow people to share great content. Higher rated content (or more shared content) gets pushed up higher on the sites and is seen by more people. How to get involved:

- Make sure your blog posts have buttons that allow for sharing (for example, the buttons from sharethis.com). Make sure that includes the top Social Media/Social Networking sites such as Facebook, LinkedIn, MySpace. Also, an email option is nice. Lastly make sure Delicious, Digg, Reddit, Linkvine, StumbleUpon and Mixx are included.

- Review the sites to see what kind of articles for your topic area rank highly. Consider this when you decide what posts you should write next

- If you decide to jump in with both feet, join the more popular sites, grow your network by inviting others to join and connecting with people on the sites.

- Find and share relevant content related to your industry.

- Once you understand the system, you can begin to introduce some of your content and encourage your network to share it or vote it up.

Promotion value: ★★★☆☆

Effort and Time: *Medium to High*

Promotion value: When done well, these sites can get a lot of attention for your content (and traffic).

Time and Effort: Enabling people to share your content via share buttons is easy. Actually building up a profile, trust from the community and a network of connections on the top sites takes time and effort. You need this foundation to get people to submit your content or to get it voted up.

Popular Social Bookmarking or Social News Sites:

www.delicious.com
www.digg.com
www.stumbleupon.com
www.Reddit.com
www.Folkd.com
www.LinkVine.com
www.mixx.com

Social Bookmarking and Social News sites are designed for sharing interesting or news-worthy content. If you can get your content to rank highly you can increase your likelihood that people will like and link to your content.

What makes Social Media so uniquely suited to promoting content online?

Social Media is designed to allow people to create, upload and share content very easily and quickly. That's why content gets passed around so quickly in Social Media platforms. Why is that?

- **Your network** – You set up your connections in advance so any content you create or share automatically is published to your network.

- **Interconnectedness between platforms** – Social Media applications can easily connect with each other making it easy to share blog posts on Facebook or Twitter, Youtube Videos on Facebook or LinkedIn or Flickr Pictures on blogs.

- **Passive sharing** – Once connected to your Social Media application (such as Facebook or LinkedIn), you can easily "like" something or join a group or even update your status or profile and it's automatically shared with your network. Some portion of your connections may also like, share or join the same thing or group spreading it quickly to all of their networks. This is how great content spreads like wildfire (or a virus - hence the term "viral")

- **Proactive sharing** – In LinkedIn or Yahoo Answers you can submit a question topic or answer a question related to an industry and can have hundreds of people view it

- **Ease of sharing from content pages** via share buttons - After I read an article I can click a share button and instantly share with either or all of my Twitter connections, Facebook connections, LinkedIn connections, Delicious connections and more.

- **Time spent on Social Media sites** - People often spend more time on Social Media sites than they do on any Web site or in their email

The Big Picture: Social Media is a key component your Web and SEO strategies

Solid Web site Foundation helps SEO and gives a better experience for visitors

Analytics to track key statistics and to adjust and improve Web site as needed

Social Media for promotion and to facilitate broad sharing and re-sharing

SEO to help you be found for your keyword phrases

Producing good content is great for SEO and can trigger sharing via Social Media

Great content to help your SEO and engage your visitors

Social Media Management Tools

With the variety of Social Media platforms out there, the way that the professionals mange their interactions, linkages between systems and content promotion activities is by using Social Media management tools.

Even if you're mainly focused on one platform such as Twitter or Facebook, these can come in very handy by helping you schedule your Tweets or Posts so you can do them in bulk as opposed to throughout each day.

Since the capabilities of these tools is constantly changing we don't attempt to describe each of them. Take a look at these popular tools – there are many others on the market as well.

- **Hootsuite**
  - www.Hootsuite.com
- **Seesmic**
  - www.Seesmic.com
- **Tweetdeck**
  - www.Tweetdeck.com
- **Ping.fm**
  - www.ping.fm
- **Social Talk**
  - www.SocialTalk.com

Wrap-up: Social Media for promotion of your content

- Social Media is means to:
  - Broadcast what's on your blog or other great content that you create
  - Connect with people where they spend time (e.g. Facebook, Twitter, LinkedIn)
  - Be less invasive and permanent than email
  - Create once and distribute broadly
  - Allow for easy sharing

- Like Blogging, it takes an investment of time and energy
  - Determine your goals
  - Start small – don't spread yourself too thin at first
  - Build your Social Media presence incrementally

- But the payoffs can be great
  - Nature of Social Media can lead to viral sharing
  - Social Media platforms provide critical exposure for your content
  - The bigger your networks and the more sites you're on, the broader your reach

In the next chapter we'll be covering the optional Pay-per-click Advertising Test

PPC tests are a quick way to see how your keywords, landing pages, content and offers are working with your target customers

Contents

A.   **Pay-per-click advertising overview**

B.   **Account and Campaign Set-up**

C.   **Ad Group set-up**

D.   **Ongoing Management and Refinement**

E.   **Lessons learned review**

Additional:

- **Keyword Match Types**

Consider a Pay-Per-Click Test of your Web site, Content and Social Media Strategy

- Once you have your SEO, Content Development and Social Media Strategies in motion, you can test the system via a Pay-per-click Advertising Test.

- As a reminder, Pay-per-Click ads show up on the top and right side of a typical Search Engine Results Page. While they get about 30% of the clicks (versus 70% for the Organic Results), they can still bring you lots of traffic quickly. Your Organic SEO work will typically take weeks or months to bear fruit).

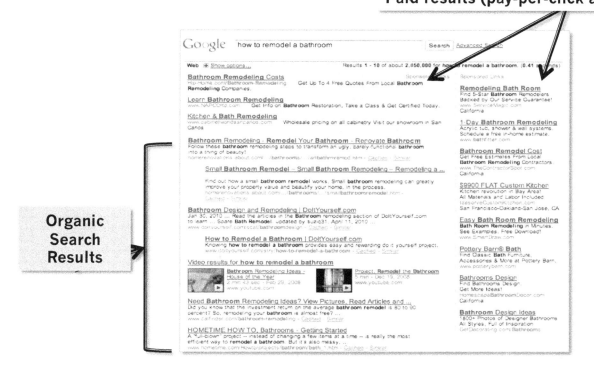

Paid results (pay-per-click ads)

Organic Search Results

Examples and descriptions in this section will be based on Google Adwords campaigns

A Pay-per-click campaign on Google is a great "reality check". It quickly puts you in front of real customers through the search results pages of Google (or Bing)

Why do a PPC test?

- PPC advertising can quickly bring significant numbers of Web searchers to any page on your site (that you choose) for the targeted keywords. This allows you to test:

  - Your keywords – do you have the right keywords? Are there other, better ones? Is there traffic for these keywords?

  - Your advertising copy or positioning – are people interested in what you have to offer or the way you position it?

  - Your Landing Pages – do people like the page and stick around or leave instantly?

  - Your Conversion Strategy – are people signing up, clicking on the link or buying the item that you had hoped they would?

How much will it cost and how long will it take?

- In a month and for between $200 and $500 you can do a PPC test that gives you some valuable insight into how searchers interact with your site. Also, if you look around in business magazines, with your Web host or online, Google is typically giving new advertisers $50 or $75 credits to try Google Adwords.

Where should I do a PPC test?

- Google gets the most search traffic so you'll get results significantly faster using Google's Adwords platform.

- The information on the following pages will apply to Adwords but Bing has similar functionality.

  - www.google.com/adwords

- On the other hand, Bing is less competitive and therefore less expensive. If you're okay to take more time to save some money, consider checking into doing the test with Bing:

  - http://advertising.microsoft.com/search-advertising

 Always be testing something. Strongly consider a pay-per-click advertising campaign to quickly test your keywords, ad positioning and landing page conversion rate. Test, modify. Test, modify.

PPC Advertising Test Steps

1 Account and Campaign Set-up

Set-up you account and launch your first campaign

2 Ad Group Set-up

Set-up ad groups within the campaign which include keywords, ads, bids and landing pages

3 Ongoing Management and Refinement

Manage and refine the campaign, ad groups, ads, keywords and bids

4 Lessons Learned Review

Document what you've learned and integrate this into your SEO and marketing efforts

 For the test it's best to start small. For example, with one campaign for one product group containing several ad groups

1 Account and Campaign Set-up

Set-up you account and launch your first campaign

Key components:

- Payment method
- Campaigns to be run
- Daily budget
- Geographic boundaries
- Languages
- Search Network and/or Content Network

- Campaign start and end date
- Times and days your ads should run
- Position Preference
- Delivery Method

Recommendations:

1. Decide which products, services or parts of your company you'll focus this test campaign on. Start simple with one product or service type.

2. Set geographic boundaries (especially if you're a local company) to limit meaningless clicks.

3. Limit your campaign financially and put an end date to make sure you stay within your budget.

4. Select the <u>Search Network</u> only for your first campaigns. This will put your ads on Google SERPS and on other partner search engines such as AOL. Deselecting the <u>Content Network</u> keeps your ads from running near content on Web sites that run Google ads (via Google's Adsense program).

5. Set times and days your ad should run - think like your customer. What times are they usually searching?

6. Delivery Method – to maximize the number of clicks you can get each day you can choose "accelerated".

7. Select to "rotate your ads evenly" if you'll be testing different ad versions (recommended) so you get equivalent numbers of impressions for each ad.. This means you will need to manually pause underperforming ads (versus having Google do it for you).

Creating a new campaign

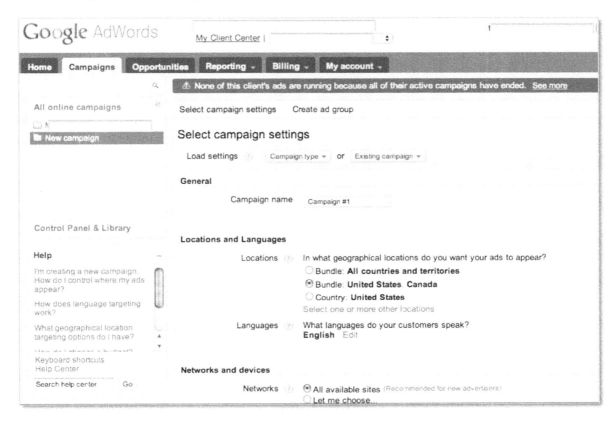

Example of selecting the Search Network and Desktop and Laptops for this test campaign

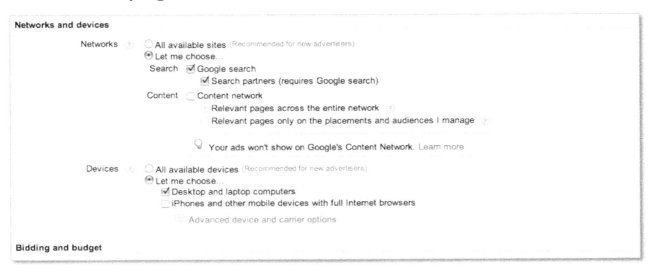

Example of Geographic Targeting

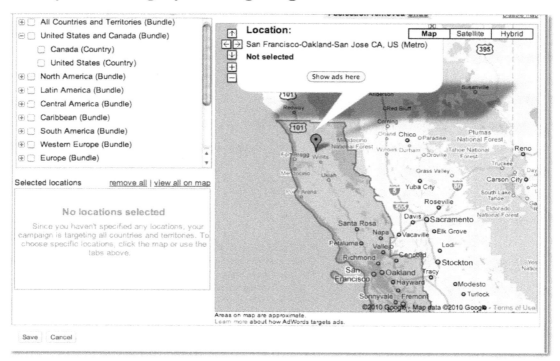

Example of Bidding Option, Daily Budget, Position Preference and Delivery Method

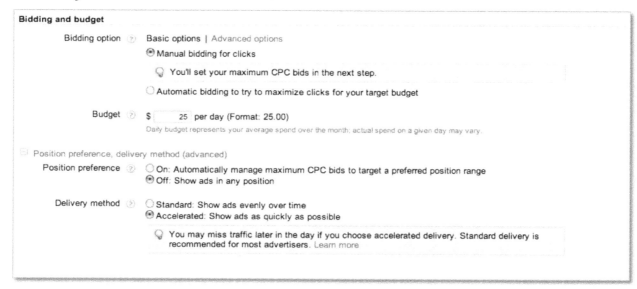

Example of setting times for ads to run

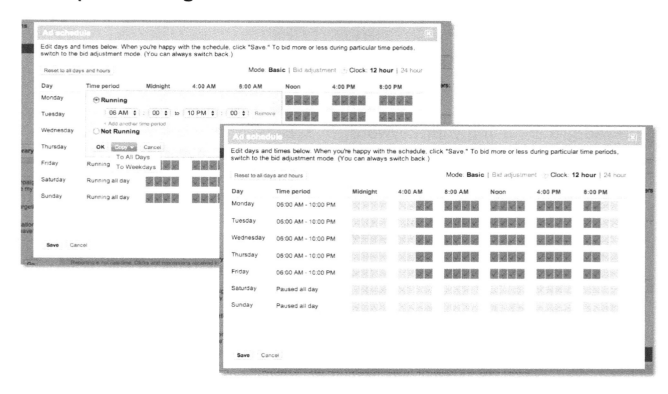

Example of Start/End Date and Ad Delivery

2

Ad Group Set-up

Set-up ad groups within the campaign which include keywords, ads, bids and landing pages

Key components:

- Ad groups using your keyword clusters
- Keywords
- Ad copy

- Bids
- Negative keywords
- Conversion tracking
- Landing pages (on your Web site)

Recommendations:

1. Create ad groups for closely related search terms. You may have several ad groups for the same product. If you are focused on specific local areas, create different ad groups for clusters of geographic search terms. Put about 5-15 keyword phrases per ad group.

2. Keywords that are unrelated to your existing ad groups should get a new ad group.

3. Make sure your ad copy includes the same keywords that you're using for that ad group.

4. Start with 2-3 different ads per ad group. As they get more impressions you can pause the ones that get significantly lower click-through rate (CTR). Then add new, slightly different variations of the "winners". You can keep testing and refining ads to improve click-through-rate (CTR).

5. Include specific offers and calls to action in your ads where possible and link your ads to relevant landing pages on your site – not always to your home page. If your ad group is "bathroom remodels" link them to a bathroom remodel page.

6. You should use the same keywords in any given ad group, the ad copy and the landing page.

7. Adjust bids so that your ads will be showing up in positions 1-5. If you bid too low you won't get clicks and this can hurt your quality score.

8. Your quality score will be higher if you get good click-through-rate (CTR) and have your keywords matched up in each ad group, ad and landing page.

9. Write down negative keywords when you're searching for positive keywords. Add negative keywords at the Campaign Level if they apply to all of your ad groups (or you can add them by ad group). Negative keywords keep your ads from showing for search terms that don't apply to your business.

10. Use and adjust the match types that you use. Broad Match will get a lot more impressions and clicks but many will be worthless to you. Phrase Match and Exact Match allow you to target more but make sure you don't limit your traffic too much! See the next page for more information on match types.

The three main keyword match types used in Google Adwords and what they mean*

In Google Adwords there are three keyword phrase matching options you can use to trigger your ads. We'll go through each and describe how they work.

Broad Match

Your ad can show for queries that contain any single word in your phrase, as well as for similar phrases, synonyms, singular/plural forms. You can see that this allows your terms to match pretty broadly and can bring a lot of untargeted traffic to your ads and Web site.

Your keyword (broad match):	Possible Matches triggering your ad:
beer mugs	beer
	mug
	buy beer mugs
	beer mug collection
	coffee mug
	beer glass

Phrase Match

If you use quotation marks, that means your keyword will be set to phrase match. In this case your ad will only match with search queries that contain those words and in that order. The phrase can contain other words as well. This is a much more targeted approach but does limit the impressions that your ad gets (the number of times it's viewed).

Your phrase:	Triggering your ad:	Won't trigger your ad:
"beer mugs	german beer mugs	mugs of beer
	buy beer mugs	beer mug
	best beer mugs	beer mug photo

Exact Match

The narrowest option. By adding brackets, your ad will only show when the exact term is used, in the same order and with no other words.

Your phrase:	Triggering your ad:	Won't trigger your ad:
[beer mugs]	beer mugs	mugs of beer
		beer mug
		beer mug photo
		buy beer mugs
		best beer mugs

* A fourth match type is "negative match which stops your ad from running if the negative word or phrase is present. See Adwords help for more details on negative keyword matching

Create a new Ad Group for your campaign

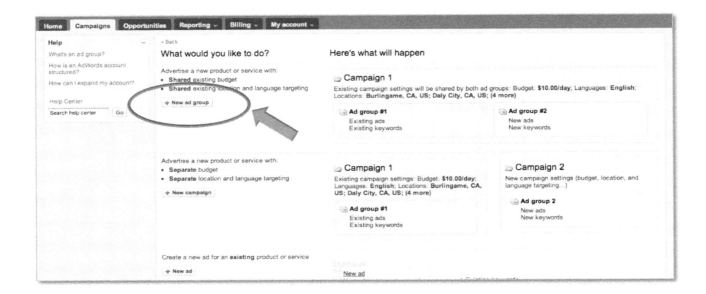

Create your first Ad

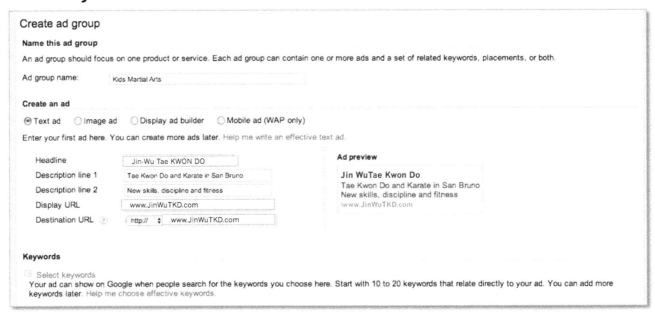

Different ways to find new keywords in Adwords

Enter Keyword Phrases hereOr select from the list here

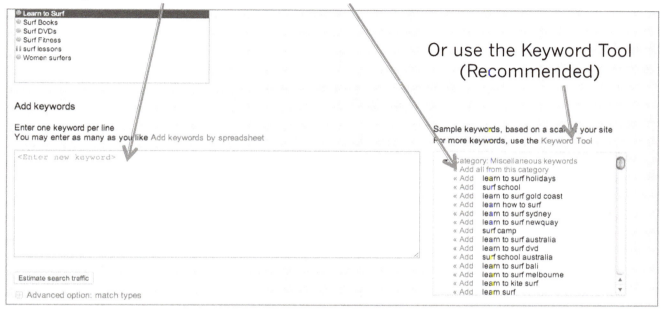

Using the Keyword Tool to find new keyword phrases and to check traffic

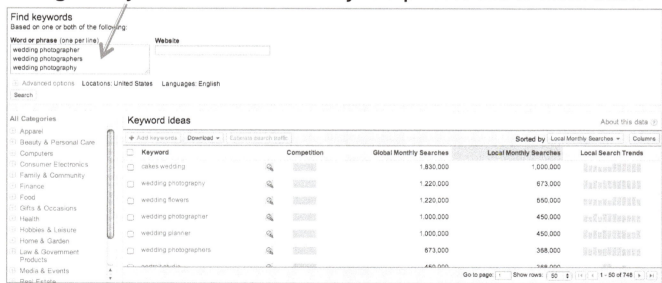

A test campaign with 6 Ad Groups

Conv. rate (many-per-click)

3.07%

0.00%
Feb 28. 2010

Mar 9, 2010

■ CTR

Edit | Change status... ▼ | More actions... ▼

		Ad group	Campaign	Status ②	Default Max. CPC	Content Max. CPC ②	Clicks	Impr.	CTR ②	Avg. CPC ②	Cost	Avg. Pos.	Conv. (1-per-click) ②	Cost / conv. (1-per-click) ②	Conv. rate (1-per-click) ②	View-through Conv. ②
☐	⦿	Wedding Photographer	March Trial Campaign	Eligible	$2.00	auto	21	1,524	1.38%	$2.77	$58.07	3.7	0	$0.00	0.00%	0
☐	⦿	Photo Journalist	March Trial Campaign	Eligible	$2.00	auto	8	217	3.69%	$2.76	$22.10	3	0	$0.00	0.00%	0
☐	⦿	Napa / Sonoma	March Trial Campaign	Eligible	$2.00	auto	1	67	1.49%	$1.95	$1.95	4.3	0	$0.00	0.00%	0
☐	⦿	Destination / Location Wedding	March Trial Campaign	Eligible	$2.00	auto	1	27	3.70%	$2.61	$2.61	4.4	0	$0.00	0.00%	0
☐	⦿	Beach Wedding 🖉	March Trial Campaign	Eligible	$2.00	auto	0	33	0.00%	$0.00	$0.00	4.5	0	$0.00	0.00%	0
☐	⦿	Creative, unique, modern, contemporary	March Trial Campaign	Eligible	$2.00	auto	0	18	0.00%	$0.00	$0.00	5.2	0	$0.00	0.00%	0
		Total - all but deleted ad groups (in all but deleted campaigns)					31	1,886	1.64%	$2.73	$84.73	3.7	0	$0.00	0.00%	0
		Total - Search ②					31	1,886	1.64%	$2.73	$84.73	3.7	0	$0.00	0.00%	0

Example of Keyword Phrases within one Ad Group

➕ Add keywords | Edit ▼ | Change status... ▼ | See search terms... ▼ | More actions... ▼

		Keyword	Status ②	Max. CPC	Qual. Score	Clicks	Impr.	CTR ②	Avg. CPC ②	Cost	Avg. Pos.
☐	⦿	**Total - all keywords**			—	37	1,260	2.94%	$5.61	$207.47	2.7
☐	⦿	"video production companies"	💬 Eligible	$7.50 〰	6/10	18	485	3.71%	$5.52	$99.30	3.1
☐	⦿	"video production services"	💬 Eligible	$8.50 〰	6/10	5	267	1.87%	$7.04	$35.22	2.6
☐	⦿	"video production costs"	💬 Eligible	$6.50	6/10	3	23	13.04%	$4.70	$14.10	2
☐	⦿	"professional video production"	💬 Eligible	$8.00 〰	5/10	2	22	9.09%	$6.65	$13.30	2.6
☐	⦿	"video production house"	💬 Eligible	$6.50	7/10	2	20	10.00%	$4.39	$8.78	3.2
☐	⦿	"product video production"	💬 Eligible	$6.50	7/10	2	15	13.33%	$4.96	$9.91	3.1
☐	⦿	"video production business"	💬 Eligible	$7.00	5/10	1	14	7.14%	$6.90	$6.90	3.4
☐	⦿	"custom video production"	💬 Eligible	$6.50	5/10	1	5	20.00%	$4.35	$4.35	1.8
☐	⦿	"media video production"	💬 Eligible	$6.50	5/10	1	7	14.29%	$5.61	$5.61	2.6
☐	⦿	"full service video production"	💬 Eligible	$6.50	5/10	1	5	20.00%	$4.20	$4.20	2.4
☐	⦿	"video production price"	💬 Eligible	$7.00	6/10	1	12	8.33%	$5.80	$5.80	2.2

3 Ongoing Management and Refinement

Manage and refine the campaign, ad groups, ads, keywords and bids

Key components:

- Adjust bids
- Pause underperforming ads
- Add, Pause, delete or move keywords

- Splinter out keywords into new ad groups
- Check reports
- Add negative keywords

Recommendations:

1. Remove (or pause) underperforming ads. Add minor refinements to the successful ads (keeping the original too) so you have 2-3 ads active at the same time in each ad group.

2. Refine keywords. Pause keywords with lots of impressions but low clicks. Add more variations for successful keywords.

3. If a keyword gets a very large amount of traffic and clicks, consider whether a more specific ad group should be made focused on that keyword.

4. Refine bids. If keywords are showing up too low (e.g. positions 6 or more), consider raising the bid to put them in positions 1-5.

5. Run reports in Adwords. My favorite is the "Search Query" report. I see what keywords have triggered my ads that are not relevant to my business. I then add these keywords as negative campaign keywords.

6. Check your analytics (Google analytics or other) to see your traffic growth, where people are spending their time on your site, which landing pages have high (or low) bounce rates and which pages have high exit rates.

7. It's a little harder to set up, but Conversion Tracking can tell you which keywords are providing conversions.

Pause (or Delete) Underperforming Ads

	Ad	Status	% Served	Clicks	Impr.	CTR	Avg. CPC	Cost	Avg. Pos.	Conv. (1-per-click)	Cost / conv. (1-per-click)	Conv. rate (1-per-click)	View-through Conv.
	Acme Photography Wedding photography. Unique and fun memories of your special event. www.Acme Photography.com	Approved	29.94%	0	153	0.00%	$0.00	$0.00	4.7	0	$0.00	0.00%	0
	Professional Wedding Photo Unique and fun wedding photography Bay Area, Napa, Sonoma, Carmel www.Acme Photography.com	Approved	32.49%	2	166	1.20%	$3.05	$6.10	4.6	0	$0.00	0.00%	0
	Wedding Photography Unique and fun wedding photography Local and Destination wedding www.Acme Photography.com	Approved	33.66%	2	172	1.16%	$2.56	$5.11	4.5	0	$0.00	0.00%	0
	Total - all deleted ads			0	20	0.00%	$0.00	$0.00	7.8	0	$0.00	0.00%	0
	Total - Search			4	511	0.78%	$2.80	$11.21	4.7	0	$0.00	0.00%	0
	Total - Content			0	0	0.00%	$0.00	$0.00	0	0	$0.00	0.00%	0
	Total - all ads			**4**	**511**	**0.78%**	**$2.80**	**$11.21**	**4.7**	**0**	**$0.00**	**0.00%**	**0**

Pause Underperforming Ad Groups (or keywords within them); Refine the high traffic and high click-through-rate Ad Groups

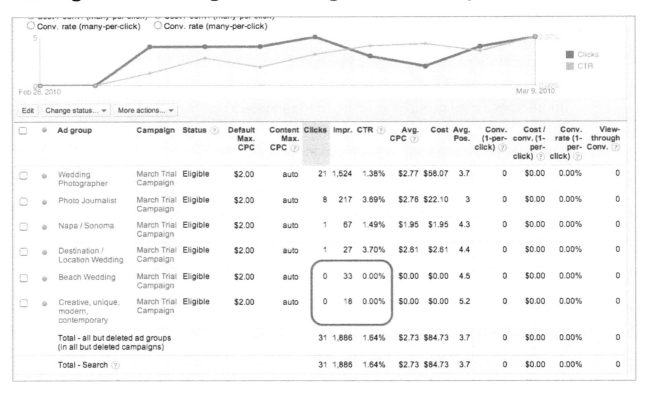

	Ad group	Campaign	Status	Default Max. CPC	Content Max. CPC	Clicks	Impr.	CTR	Avg. CPC	Cost	Avg. Pos.	Conv. (1-per-click)	Cost / conv. (1-per-click)	Conv. rate (1-per-click)	View-through Conv.
	Wedding Photographer	March Trial Campaign	Eligible	$2.00	auto	21	1,524	1.38%	$2.77	$58.07	3.7	0	$0.00	0.00%	0
	Photo Journalist	March Trial Campaign	Eligible	$2.00	auto	8	217	3.69%	$2.76	$22.10	3	0	$0.00	0.00%	0
	Napa / Sonoma	March Trial Campaign	Eligible	$2.00	auto	1	67	1.49%	$1.95	$1.95	4.3	0	$0.00	0.00%	0
	Destination / Location Wedding	March Trial Campaign	Eligible	$2.00	auto	1	27	3.70%	$2.61	$2.61	4.4	0	$0.00	0.00%	0
	Beach Wedding	March Trial Campaign	Eligible	$2.00	auto	0	33	0.00%	$0.00	$0.00	4.5	0	$0.00	0.00%	0
	Creative, unique, modern, contemporary	March Trial Campaign	Eligible	$2.00	auto	0	18	0.00%	$0.00	$0.00	5.2	0	$0.00	0.00%	0
	Total - all but deleted ad groups (in all but deleted campaigns)					31	1,886	1.64%	$2.73	$84.73	3.7	0	$0.00	0.00%	0
	Total - Search					31	1,886	1.64%	$2.73	$84.73	3.7	0	$0.00	0.00%	0

4

Lessons Learned

Document what you've learned and integrate into SEO and marketing efforts

Key components:

- Which keywords and ads brought traffic
- Which keywords and ads brought conversions
- How competitive the market is for your main search terms
- Which landing pages performed well
- Which offers or conversions were effective
- Which negative keywords are required

Recommendations:

1. Refine your overall target keyword phrases and keyword clusters based on what you learn from your Adwords test

2. Integrate these adjusted keywords into your Web, Social Media, sales and marketing materials

3. Emphasize or improve successful offers; discontinue those that were unsuccessful

4. Determine if the ROI was positive for the initial campaign; if so, consider running it again on a larger scale

5. Consider running additional campaigns for other products or services; make sure you don't make your campaigns too complex to actively manage

6. Document your negative keywords for use in future campaigns

- In the this chapter we highlighted the key steps of a Pay-per-click Advertising Test, discussed recommendations for each step and provided a behind-the-scenes look at some screenshots from actual campaigns.

- For a PPC test, make sure you limit your financial exposure with spending limits and follow the recommendations for each step. You can learn a lot from these tests, even if you only run it for 3-4 weeks.

- In the next chapter we'll be wrapping up the boot camp with a review of the Direction SEO process.

Chapter 11. Conclusion

Be strategic in your SEO in order
to beat out the competition

Review of the 10 Steps of the Direction SEO Process

Rather than using tricks, gimmicks or short-lived strategies, good SEO that will have staying power needs to be based on a sound strategy that crosses multiple disciplines. Make sure you use a process flow such as the one below to make sure you cover all of the key steps.

Direction SEO 10 Step Process

1. Tie your SEO Plans to Company Strategy

2. Understand your Customers and Competitors

3. Determine your Target Keywords

4. Get your Web site and Analytics Foundation in Place

5. Develop your SEO Balanced Scorecard

6. Do On-Page SEO Fundamentals

7. Do Off-Page SEO, mainly Inbound Link Building

8. Create Compelling Web site Content

9. Use Social Media to Drive Awareness and Links

10. Optional: Do a Paid Search Test for Keywords, Conversions, Positioning

Review of the 10 Steps of the Direction SEO Process

1) Tie your SEO Plans to your Company Strategy

Align your efforts so you get the full benefit of the SEO work and waste as little time as possible on unproductive activities

2) Understand your Customers and Competitors

Understanding your customers, how they buy and why they buy will help you with your SEO efforts. Learning from competitors is important and can be eye-opening.

3) Determine your Target Keywords

Make sure you're hitting the mark with your target keywords. Optimizing your SEO on the wrong keywords is a waste of effort and money.

4) Get your Web site and Analytics Foundation in Place

These are fundamental things that need to be in place – like "table stakes" in poker

5) Develop your SEO Balanced Scorecard

You need to track key metrics to know if you're making progress with your SEO efforts

6) Do On-Page SEO Fundamentals

Take care of On-page SEO Fundamentals and build these into your company processes

7) Do Off-Page SEO, mainly Inbound Link Building

Getting quality links to your pages is the most important factor for ranking highly in search engines

8) Create Compelling Web site Content

Compelling content helps your customers and is a key part of getting people to link to your site

9) Use Social Media to Drive Awareness and Links

Social Media is the most effective way to spread the word about your great content

10) Optional: Do a Paid Search Test for Keywords, Conversions, Positioning

Doing a quick Google Adwords campaign is the fastest way to battle test your keywords, ad copy, content, landing pages and conversions

Next Up...Appendices

Appendices:
Table of Contents

Templates, Checklists and Key Steps Guides

1 **Tie Your SEO Work to the Company Strategy**

☐ Pick company priorities to focus your initial SEO efforts on:

  ▪ Company or Division strategic priorities

  ▪ Key products or services

  ▪ Target segments

☐ Document key sales, marketing, web or Social Media activities that need to be linked to SEO

☐ Make sure that SEO is considered a key part of the overall company strategy

2 **Understand your Customers and Competitors**

Customers

☐ Choose highest priority customer segments

☐ Complete personas for target segments

☐ Understand how target segments search and which keywords they use

Competitors

☐ Review the Web sites, blogs and Social Media sites of known offline competitors

☐ Check obvious keywords and identify companies ranking high in the search engines ("online competitors")

☐ Compete competitor template for top competitors

☐ Set up Google Alerts or subscribe to key competitor and industry blogs via RSS (or email)

3 Develop Your Target Keyword List

- ☐ Pick a high priority product or service category or customer segment to focus on first

- ☐ Collect a preliminary keyword list by:
  - ▪ Listing out keywords
  - ▪ Brainstorming
  - ▪ Talking to customers

- ☐ Refine your keyword list by:
  - ▪ Looking at competitor sites
  - ▪ Finding more keywords by doing searches in search engines
  - ▪ Using keyword tools for new keywords and to get quantitative date

- ☐ Make a final keyword list including major Keyword Clusters with Main Keywords and Supporting Keywords (this list can continue to be refined as you use it and learn more)

- ☐ Optional – collect negative keywords, slang, misspellings and potential niche or long tail keyword phrases

- ☐ Communicate the final list to any relevant stakeholders (marketing, IT, sales collateral creators, web designers, etc.)

4 Get Your Web site and Analytics In Place

- ☐ Evaluate your current Web site technology for the ability to implement SEO

- ☐ Make a decision on a go-forward Web site technology that is SEO-friendly and allows for easy addition of content

- ☐ Develop a logical Web site site map that groups related sections together with inter-linking between those related pages

- ☐ Evaluate whether or not a domain name change is needed

- ☐ Choose a reputable web hosting company (if needed)

- ☐ Select and implement a Web site analytics package

5 Develop an SEO Balanced Scorecard

- [ ] Select the set of metrics that you will track in the short term
- [ ] Select metrics you would like to track in the future
- [ ] Select tools to use and set baseline for important metrics:
    - [ ] Pages Indexed
    - [ ] Inbound Links
    - [ ] Web site traffic
    - [ ] Conversions
    - [ ] Search Engine Rank for top keywords
    - [ ] Current Google Toolbar PageRank
    - [ ] Other key metrics: _____
- [ ] Pick a person to review these and set a regular frequency to check the metrics

6 Do On-Page SEO Actions

- [ ] Create keyword-rich unique page titles for each of your key pages
- [ ] Populate your Web site with keyword-rich content (See "Develop Web site and Blog Content")
- [ ] Validate that your Web site has simple HTML navigation for all key pages
- [ ] Create at least one very targeted landing page for your area of focus for your SEO efforts
- [ ] Validate that your URLs are search-engine friendly (as much as possible)
- [ ] Check for missing or changed pages and put 301 redirects in place for those
- [ ] Make sure that you have keyword phrases in header tags and bold or strong text (as appropriate)
- [ ] Make sure to link between related
- [ ] Link out to authority sites you reference
- [ ] Create meta description tags with appealing "marketing copy" for key pages of your Web site
- [ ] Create at least one video and optimize it with a good title, surrounding text and page title
- [ ] Optimize your other files including pictures and presentations with keyword-rich filenames and link anchor text (e.g. not "download" as anchor text)

7   Do Off-Page SEO Tactics / Link-Building

☐ Check your site's current inbound links – document any issues with links (e.g. bad anchor text or linking to wrong page)

☐ Document target pages for getting links:

    ☐ Links that competitors have that also make sense for your company

    ☐ Key industry blogs, directories, associations or news sites

    ☐ Other company sites

    ☐ Partner or customer Web sites

    ☐ General directories or internet yellow pages sites

    ☐ Locally-focused sites, directories or social review sites

    ☐ Employee sites or company Social Media sites

☐ Do basic link-building to get links up on target sites over time

☐ Develop relationships with key industry Web site or blog owners

☐ Develop a "content strategy" to attract links

8   Develop Web site and Blog Content

☐ Make your Web site content SEO-friendly and keyword rich based on your target keywords and Keyword Clusters

☐ Develop a blogging strategy

    ☐ Brainstorm a blog "angle" and potential blog post topics

    ☐ Develop a first draft of editorial calendar

    ☐ Put an "editor" in charge and set a calendar or posting cadence

    ☐ Write the first blog posts; respond to any comments

☐ Develop an educational content strategy

    ☐ Research what's available and what competitors are doing

    ☐ Brainstorm ideas for filling gaps or providing unique, useful educational content

    ☐ Plan and develop educational content (video, articles, checklists, etc.)

9 Develop a Social Media Content Promotion Strategy

☐ Do your Social Media sites homework:

  ▪ Find out where your customers congregate or what Social Media platforms they use

  ▪ See what your competitors are doing

  ▪ Sign up for personal accounts to test and learn more about potential Social Media sites

☐ Pick your 1-2 Social Media sites, set up company accounts and make connections to customers, partners, potential customers and other industry stakeholders

☐ Tie Content to Social Media

  ▪ Promote and share content via Social Media sites

  ▪ Comment on industry blogs and, where it makes sense, provide information or a link to your content

  ▪ Engage with your customers in Social Media sites where appropriate

☐ Make sure you have a plan in place to generate content and to share content from other industry sources

10 Optional: Pay-per-click Test

☐ Sign up for Google Adwords or Bing Search Advertising

☐ Utilize Keyword Clusters to set up Ad Groups and populate with keywords

☐ Make sure to be conscious of:

  ▪ Limiting daily and campaign cost

  ▪ Setting geographic boundaries and appropriate run times

  ▪ Match types for keywords – make sure you use phrase match and exact match where possible to limit irrelevant clicks

  ▪ Making sure Ad Groups include related keywords and that ads are focused on those keywords

  ▪ Send people to landing pages relevant for the keywords they're searching on

  ▪ Use negative keywords to limit irrelevant clicks

  ▪ Test more than one version of ad in each ad group

☐ Manage and refine your ads, keywords and bids regularly

☐ Learn about the keywords, conversions and ad copy and bring these lessons into your SEO work

Customer Persona Template (part 1)

Customer Persona (part 1)	
Persona Title:	
Example Customer's Name (made up)	His/Her Current Occupation
Age, locale, marital status, kids, education level	Why do they want your products or services?
How/Where do they find your company or products/services?	What compels them to buy your products versus the competitors'?
What benefits do they get from using your products/services?	What objections might they have?

Customer Persona (part 2)	
Persona Title:	
Main Products Purchased	Sites, blogs or Social Media sites they frequent
Information they want from us (for use in content creation)	Create a landing page for them? What's on it? What conversions?
How/Where do they search?	What keyword phrases would they use?
Key marketing messages for this group	Other notes or questions

Competitor Evaluation Template

Competitor Evaluation Template			
Competitor name and URL:			
Keyword phrases they're ranking highly for and target keywords	Good content on site and Blog	Conversions targeted	Social Media Usage
Keyword ideas for your SEO	Content/Blog ideas	Conversion ideas	Social Media ideas

Keyword list Development Steps

☐ **1) Determine which Section of your Web site and which Products/Services you'll focus on first**

- For your homepage the keyword phrases can be more generic with more specific keywords for product/service sections
- Focus on one major section at a time

☐ **2) List out the Obvious Keywords for that product, product type, brand**

- Product, product type, industry, brands, problems solved
- Local keywords – cities, counties served or targeted

☐ **3) Brainstorm additional potential keyword phrases**

- Think like a customer – what would you type to find your products, services or company?

☐ **4) Interview customers, sales or other stakeholders**

- How do they search?
- What keywords do they use?

☐ **5) Bring in other external data for more ideas; purge irrelevant keywords from your master list**

- What keywords are the competitors using on their pages?
- What do you see when you do some searches using the keywords you've already collected?
- Your Web site analytics – what are people using now to find your site?
- Look at blogs, forums, YouTube, etc.

☐ **6) Make "Keyword Clusters"- cluster similar keywords into logical groupings**

- Make groups of related keywords, including high traffic "Main Keyword Phrases" and "Supporting Keyword Phrases"

☐ **7) Use keyword tools to get quantitative data and related keywords**

- Use Google Keyword Tool or other keyword tools to get traffic estimates

☐ **8) Finalize clusters**

- Based on the traffic and also keyword relevance, adjust your clusters
- Designate Main Keyword Phrases and Supporting Keyword Phrases

☐ **9) Document negative keywords, common misspellings, slang and potential niche keywords for future use**

- Negative keywords are words you found that are very irrelevant for your company
- Relevant, niche keywords can be good for blog posts, whitepapers or videos

☐ **10) Utilize your Keyword Clusters in your SEO, advertising and Social Media activities**

- Keeping related keywords together in sections of your Web site helps emphasize what that page is focused on

Web site Positive Attributes Checklist

(Check all that apply)

+'s

- ☐ I have an attractive site

- ☐ My site has the type of content my customers would expect or seek out

- ☐ My site also has some unique elements or content

- ☐ My site has clear navigation paths

- ☐ My site has clear "calls to action" – learn more here, buy here, sign-up here

- ☐ My site can be quickly updated on the fly to add new messaging, to launch a new campaign or to add a customer testimonial or content

- ☐ I have a blog that is part of my site and I am not linking to a blog hosted elsewhere

- ☐ I can easily integrate multimedia into my site (video, audio, pictures)

- ☐ I can integrate buttons or badges for people to share my content or to follow me on Social Media platforms such as Facebook, Twitter or LinkedIn

- ☐ My site that has fairly new HTML structure (it's recent and is compliant with W3C standards – www.w3c.org)

- ☐ I use my own URL only (it is www.MySite.com not www.MySite.blogspot.com)

- ☐ Each page has a unique address (ideally not numbers but with words)

  Not: www.mycompany.com and .com/132

  But www.mycompany.com and .com/super-product

- ☐ It's clear how I'll convert customers when they arrive at my site

Web site: Negative Attributes Checklist

(Check all that apply)

—'s

- ☐ My site is static – the content is rarely updated

- ☐ I can't change the site easily – I need to hire an expensive developer and it's a painful process

- ☐ It's hard to add pictures or video to my site

- ☐ I can't easily access my meta tags such as meta page title or meta page description to update them

- ☐ I can't easily add buttons to share my content on Social Media sites such as Facebook, Twitter and Delicious

- ☐ I can't easily add buttons for people to follow me on Twitter, Facebook or LinkedIn

- ☐ My blog is hosted on a separate platform than my Web site

- I don't have clear "calls to action" for customers to contact me, inquire about products/services, access white papers or sign up for my email newsletter

- ☐ My Web site HTML is old – it was designed more than 3 years ago and hasn't been updated since then

- ☐ My site always shows the same URL no matter what page you click on

- ☐ My site is hosted on a platform and my URL includes the platform's name– i.e. www.MySite.wordpress.com/

- ☐ I have advertising which may take people to other sites or that makes the site look less professional

- ☐ My site is unattractive or old-looking

- ☐ I have some pages that are basically empty of content

- ☐ It takes multiple clicks to get to some of my important content

- ☐ I don't have an easy navigation method to all of my key content

- ☐ I have branding from my Web site hosting company on the site

- ☐ I have links on my site that are from link-trading

What to look for in choosing a CMS

☐ Popularity – you want to choose a CMS that is popular because that means developers will continue to improve the platform, templates and plug-ins

☐ Ease of use – try out demos or review training to see if it is easy to use for the people who will be updating your site; the interface should be easy to understand

☐ Contains key functionality that you need for your business (e.g. manages pictures well if you're in the photography business, handles video well if that's important to you, allows you to manage multiple products or integrates with a shopping cart if needed, etc.)

☐ Allows you to add new functionality via plug-ins or add-ons

☐ Allows you to do the basic On-page SEO tactics including:

- Customizing URLs with keywords; those URLs should be stable over time (not changing dynamically)

- Adding Page Titles and Meta Descriptions

- Adding Alt Tags to pictures

- Adding Headers and Bold or Strong text

- Adding virtually unlimited amounts of content or pages

☐ Should have good documentation, training and support

☐ Allows you to use your own URL and Host

☐ Contains the ability to integrate an analytics platform such as Google Analytics, Piwick or others

Example of the summary page of an SEO Balanced Scorecard

Pages Indexed/Inbound Links

	Last month	This month	% improvement
Pages indexed			
•Google	49	61	19%
•Bing	36	43	21%
•Yahoo	47	51	7%
Inbound Links by PageRank:			
•PR8-10 pages	2	3	50%
•PR5-7 pages	3	5	83%
•PR2-4 pages	12	14	18%
•PR0-1 pages	27	31	11%

Keywords/Ranking

Number of Keyword ranking in:	Last month	This month	Goal / % of goal
Positions 1-10	5	8	10
Positions 11-20	3	6	5
Positions 20-30	7	12	2
Positions 30-40	10	15	16
Positions 40-50	23	25	22
Not ranking in top 50	43	40	36

Website Traffic

	Last month	This month	% improvement
Total Traffic	1,204	1,453	15%
Traffic Sources:			
Search	432	543	11%
Referrals	540	567	2%
Direct	276	285	2%
Avg. time on site	2:34	3:45	23%
Avg. pages visited	3.1	3.6	12%
Avg. bounce rate	45%	36%	25%

Conversions/Social Media

	Last month	This month	% improvement
Twitter:			
•Tweets	64	75	18%
•Followers	345	465	16%
Facebook:			
• Members	234	245	2%
YouTube:			
•Views	33	23	-35%
Newsletter Subscribers	275	245	-9%
New Leads	7	14	100%
Internet-influenced Sales	$235K	$301K	16%

PR* = Toolbar PageRank

Set up your SEO Balanced Scorecard:

Use this template to pick your metrics and how you'll measure them (refer to the example if unsure where to start). Feel free to start with some basic metrics at first (traffic, keyword rankings, inbound links, pages indexed, newsletter sign-ups, etc.)

Metric category:	
Metrics:	Measurement tool or methodology:

Metric category:	
Metrics:	Measurement tool or methodology:

Metric category:	
Metrics:	Measurement tool or methodology:

Metric category:	
Metrics:	Measurement tool or methodology:

SEO Essentials Checklist

Use this to review the SEO essential topics. Many of them require ongoing work but this can help you make sure you've at least reviewed or started on many of the key areas.

SEO Essentials	Import ance?	Addressed?	Status or comments:
1. Attract quality inbound links	(must do)		
2. Unique page title for all pages	(must do)		
3. A big helping of keyword-rich textual content	(must do)		
4. Simple HTML navigation versus (or in addition to) JavaScript or Flash navigation	(must do)		
5. Use of landing pages 100% focused on 1-3 target keyword phrases	(must do)		
6. Search Friendly URLs for your Web site	(must do)		
7 Internal linking in your using good anchor text	(must do)		
8. 301 Redirects for missing pages or changed URLs	(must do)		
9. Quality web host with excellent uptime	(must do)		
10. Create an XML site map and submit it to Google and Bing	(good to do)		
11. Keyword Phrases in header tags and bold/ strong	(good to do)		
12. Meta description tags for each page of your Web site	(good to do)		
13. Use video, optimize it and create a video site map	(good to do)		
14. Optimize your files including video, images, PDFs, audio files and presentations	(good to do)		
15, Register your site with Google Webmaster Central and Bing Webmaster Center	(good to do)		
16. Register your site with Google Places and Bing Local	(good to do)		
17. Keywords in domain name	(optional)		
18. Improve page load speed where possible	(optional)		
19. Meta keyword tags on key pages of your Web site	(optional)		

Content development checklist

Use this checklist to get you started on improving current content and developing new content for SEO purposes

▪ Your Web site content:

☐ Used target keyword phrases in all main pages of key Web site content (as well as in page titles, headers, picture alt tags, internal links)

☐ Utilized geographic keywords and niche-specific keywords to narrow your competition

☐ Expanded your content so each page has at least 200 words

☐ Linked internally to related content

▪ Your blog content:

☐ Set up a blog which is on the same domain as your Web site (e.g. www.MySite.com/Blog).

☐ Decided on a tone and goal for the blog (e.g. what is the purpose, how will people find it helpful or interesting, what types of content will you create, what types of industry content will you share or comment on?)

☐ Developed a draft editorial calendar for at least the first 1-2 months; determined a target frequency for posting and selected someone to make sure content gets created

☐ You've written and posted your first blog post

▪ Your Educational Content:

☐ You've analyzed the educational content (mainly informal educational content) in the industry and found some potential gaps

☐ You've brainstormed ideas on what type of content to create and what formats (e.g. video, article, an educational series of blog posts, a mini-class, Webinar, a series of emails)

☐ You've selected your first topic and have begun writing

List of Tools

Tools List by Chapter:

Chapter 3: Develop your Keyword List:

■ **Keyword Research and Discovery Tools (free):**

- **Adwords Keyword Tool** (free with Adwords account) - http://www.adwords.google.com/

- **Google Keyword Tool External** - https://adwords.google.com/select/KeywordToolExternal

■ **Keyword Research and Discovery Tools (paid):**

- **WordTracker** - http://www.wordtracker.com/

- **Keyword Discovery** - http://www.keyworddiscovery.com/

- **Wordstream** - http://www.wordstream.com/

Chapter 4: Web site and Analytics:

■ **Content Management Systems:**

- **Wordpress** – www.wordpress.org

- **Joomla** – www.Joomla.org

- **Drupal** – www.Drupal.org

- **CMS Made Simple** – www.cmsmadesimple.com

■ **Analytics Tools (Free)**

- **Google Analytics** - www.google.com/analytics

- **Piwik** - www.piwik.org

■ **Analytics Tools (paid):**

- **Webtrends** – www.webtrends.com

- **Omniture** – www.omniture.com

- **Coremetrics** – www.coremetrics.com

■ **Web Host that works well with Wordpress (self-hosted):**

- **Blue Host** (affiliate link) - http://www.BlueHost.Com/track/RMM

Chapter 5: Develop your SEO Balanced Scorecard

- **Checking Pages Indexed:**

  - **Google** – www.google.com - Enter the following in the search bar: site:MyCompany.com and you can also use site: www.MyCompany.com (no spaces after "site:")

  - **Bing** – www.bing.com - Enter the same info as above for Google

  - **Yahoo! Site Explorer** – https://siteexplorer.search.yahoo.com/mysites

- **Checking Inbound Links:**

  - **Link Diagnosis** – www.linkdiagnosis.com - Plugin for Firefox browser

  - **Yahoo! Site Explorer** – https://siteexplorer.search.yahoo.com/mysites - Hit explore URL and select "except from this domain"

  - **SEO Pro Link Checker** - http://seopro.com.au/free-seo-tools/link-checker/

  - **Majestic SEO** – www.majesticseo.com

  - **AdGoogroo Link Insight** - http://www.adgooroo.com/

  - **SEOMoz Toolbar** (for Chrome browser) - http://www.seomoz.org/seo-toolbar

- **Checking Search Engine Ranks for Keywords:**

  - **SEO Book Rank Checker** (free Firefox plugin) - http://tools.seobook.com/firefox/rankchecker/

  - **SEO Cockpit** (inexpensive Web-based tool) - www.SEOcockpit.com

  - **SEOMoz RankTracker** (paid membership required)- http://www.seomoz.org/rank-tracker

  - **SEO Power Suite – Rank Tracker** (free and paid versions) - http://www.link-assistant.com/rank-tracker/

- **Checking PageRank of your site or others:**

  - **Google Toolbar** (for Internet Explorer or Firefox) - http://toolbar.google.com

  - **SEOBook Toolbar** (for Firefox)- http://tools.seobook.com/firefox/seo-for-firefox.html

  - **Webrank Toolbar** for Firefox - https://addons.mozilla.org/en-US/firefox/addon/52177/

Chapter 6: 19 SEO Essentials

- **Local Business Listings in Google/Bing:**
  - **Google Places:** http://www.google.com/local/add/BusinessCenter
  - **Bing Local:** https://ssl.bing.com/listings/ListingCenter.aspx

Chapter 9: Promoting your Content via Social Media

- **Social Media Sites:**
  - Social Networking - Facebook, MySpace
  - Business Social Networking - LinkedIn. Plaxo
  - Photo Sharing - Flickr, Picasa, Photobucket
  - Video Sharing - YouTube, Vimeo
  - Social Reviewing –
    - Yelp!, Rate it All, Kudzu.com, Angie's List, Merchant Circle, Yellow Bot, Brown Book, Service Magic, Judy's Book, Praized, City Voter, Insider Pages
  - Microblogging - Twitter, Yammer
  - Social Bookmarking/Social News
    - www.delicious.com, www.digg.com, www.stumbleupon.com, www.Reddit.com, www.Folkd.com, www.LinkVine.com, www.mixx.com

- **Social Media Management Tools:**
  - Hootsuite - www.Hootsuite.com
  - Seesmic - www.Seesmic.com
  - Tweetdeck - www.Tweetdeck.com
  - Ping.fm - www.ping.fm
  - Social Talk - www.SocialTalk.com

- **Creating and Submitting XML Sitemaps:**
  - **For help in creating an XML sitemap**: http://www.sitemaps.org/
  - **Submit sitemap via Google Webmaster Central**: http://www.google.com/places/
  - **Submit sitemap via Bing Webmaster Center**: https://ssl.bing.com/listings/ListingCenter.aspx

- **Creating a Video Sitemap:**
  - **For information on creating video sitemaps:**
    - http://www.google.com/support/webmasters/bin/answer.py?hl=en&answer=80472

- **Measuring your Web site's page load speed:**
  - **Page Speed Firefox Browser Plugin** - http://code.google.com/speed/page-speed/
  - **ySlow Firefox Browser Plugin** http://developer.yahoo.com/yslow/

- **How to view a Web site's code:**
  - On the menu at the top of the browser start with "View".
    - **Internet Explorer**: View > Source
    - **Safari:** View > Source
    - **Firefox:** View > Page Source
    - **Chrome:** View > Developer > View Source

Chapter 10: Pay-per-Click Advertising Test

- **Pay-per-click advertising platforms:**
  - **Adwords -** www.google.com/adwords
  - **Microsoft Adcenter -** http://advertising.microsoft.com/search-advertising

Glossary of Key Terms

Ad Group	In pay per click advertising (such as Google Adwords), a grouping that contains ads that will display in the "sponsored results" section when a certain set of keywords are typed in the search engine
address bar	In a Web browser such as Internet Explorer or Firefox, the area where the Web site address can be typed in (or where the address will be displayed when a user navigates to a Web page)
AOL	Previously an Internet powerhouse, AOL has fallen on hard times. its search engine is #5 but its share is miniscule compared to that of Google's. Also, it gets its search results from Google so for the purposes of SEO, it can be considered part of Google.
article marketing	Submitting written articles to Web sites which allow that article to be used by any Web site but only in its complete form (including any credits or links to the writers Web site). It's considered "marketing" because your articles can potentially get you leads or may pass "Link Juice" back to your site.
Ask.com	Previously called AskJeeves (at askjeeves.com), the #4 search engine in terms of search market share.
authority	A site can increase its "authority" in the eyes of the search engines by getting quality inbound links from high ranking or authority Web pages
backlink	A link to a page on your Web site. Also called an "inbound link".
Bing	Microsoft's new search engine, replacing Microsoft Live Search. As of August 2010 it provides the engine results Yahoo's search so (combined with Yahoo) it's now #2 in search share.
Black Hat SEO	People who perform SEO that the Search Engines consider undesirable. Black Hat SEOs are typically trying to game the system with search engines to improve the ranks of Web sites they own (or their customer's sites). If search engines consider your site to be using black hat techniques, it can ban the site from their index, either permanently or for a period of time.
blended search	The move by search engines to include various types of information in the search results including maps, stock prices, video thumbnails, Social Media information, news articles and (of course) links to standard Web pages.
blog	A blog (or weblog) is a site that includes articles or other content that is updated on a periodic basis. The style is usually less formal than a typical Web site and the structure is more centered around being able to find the most recent content as well a archives of the content by time or topic. There are many free blog software platforms available so a new one is very easy to start.
bounce rate	In Web site analytics a typical measure is bounce rate. This is the number of people who arrive at your site and leave from the same page (without exploring other pages of your site). The lower the bounce rate you have for your Web site, the better.
cached	The saved copy of a Web page that a search engine keeps in its servers; this may be different from the content on the current Web page at that same address (i.e. if the page has been updated by the owner)

217

campaign   In pay per click advertising, a campaign is the major grouping for a certain advertising effort. A campaign will include several ad groups, each of which includes sets of keywords and ads.

canonical tag   A tag introduced by the search engines to help reduce the number of duplicate pages and content in their indexes. The canonical tag allows people to set (on each page) which address the search engines should use for the main (canonical) address for that page. This helps because the same page can usually be displayed for more than one address (e.g. www.MySite.com and http://MySite.com).

click-through rate In pay per click advertising, the number of times a keyword or ad is clicked on compared to the number of times that ad or keyword has been viewed by a searcher. A high click-through rate is considered better than a low one. Often abbreviated to "CTR".

content   Written, graphical, video or pictorial work on a Web site or Social Media platform. Content can be created by the owner of the Web site or Social Media site or by the users. Content can be an article, a status post, a description of something with a link, a picture, a video or any other work designed to inform, entertain or teach.

conversion   The process of converting a person to a deeper stage in your selling process. For example, a first time visitor can be come your newsletter subscriber. This can be counted as a conversion. Other conversions can include: Downloading a white paper, viewing a video, signing up for something, purchasing something, requesting more information about something or signing up for your Facebook page or Twitter feed.

CPC   Cost per click. The amount an advertiser needs to pay (in Google Adwords) for each time someone clicks on their text advertisement (see Google Adwords).

CSS   CSS = Cascading Style Sheets. A technology for designing Web sites using style sheets to control the structure and look and feel separately from the content.

CTR   See click-through rate

destination URL   In pay per click advertising, the Web page address that you will be sending searchers to if they click on your ad. URL = Web page address.

directory   A directory is a listing of Web sites, usually with links to those sites and often with descriptions. Quality directories often produce good inbound links with high SEO value. Examples include the Open Directory at www.DMOZ.org, the Yahoo Directory, the Best of the Web Directory (www.bestoftheweb.com) or industry-specific directories such as the AIA (American Institute of Architect) list of members.

display ad   A display advertisement is a graphic ad which can include pictures, color and can include simple movement or animations.

diy   Do It Yourself - DIY is doing something yourself versus buying something ready-made or paying someone else to make it for you.

duplicate content	Web pages that are considered to have the same content as other Web pages. It's believed that Google makes efforts to de-prioritize or penalize pages that have content that is the same as other pages (either on the same Web site or on other Web sites)
Facebook PPC	Pay per click advertising available on Facebook that allows advertisers to select the demographics or other aspects of their target customers (such as what company they work for or what companies they are fans of). The ads show up to the right of the users news feed.
Flash	Adobe's software technology which enables the creation of attractive animation or video content. Web sites can also be created using Flash. For SEO, Flash Web sites are not considered as desirable as HTML or CSS Web sites. This is because Flash isn't as easily read by the search engine spiders and it doesn't normally include all of the different code such as Meta Description Tag, Page Title or Canonical Tag that HTML and CSS can include.
Google	The largest search engine in the US (and much of the world) in terms of share of searches
Google Adsense	A platform that allows individual Web site owners (or companies) to include ads from Google advertisers near their content (see Google Content Network)
Google Adwords	Google's pay per click advertising platform. Any company or person can sign up and advertise their products or services (excluding some advertisers such as liquor, drugs, guns and pornography). The ads can be text ads, image ads or animated ads. The ads can be placed on SERPs (Search Engine Results Pages) or on sites with content (e.g. on a Web site such as CNN.com). Although the platform is mostly pay per click, there are some lesser-used options such as Pay for Action (e.g. pay when someone makes a purchase or signs up for something) or CPM (cost per 1000 views).
Google Analytics	Google's free Web site analytics platform.
Google Content Network	A network of Web sites that host Google text ads near their content (they sign up to be on the Content Network via Google's Adsense program and take a cut of the payments for each click). If you advertise on Google's Adwords platform you can advertise on all or one of three areas: 1) Google's search engine 2) Google's Search Network (other search engines that use Google's search results or 3) Google's Content Network (see above). The Content Network is typically considered trickier to use than the Google's search engine or the Search Network.
Google Search Network	Other search engines that utilize Google's search results and also allow for advertisements from Google Adwords. The search network typically has lower traffic than Google's search engine but also has lower Cost Per Click for advertising (CPC).
Grey Hat SEO	A person who does SEO that pushes the limits of "white hat" and comes close to crossing into black hat SEO
hidden text	Putting content that will help the site rank highly on a site in a way that it is hidden from the visitor. This way the search engine reads the content but the user doesn't.

hyperlink	Also called "link". Making a link from a Web page, email or search result page to a Web page, video, document or Social Media site page. Links are now used by search engines to help them determine a site's authority and relevance for a particular query.
impressions	An impression is when someone views an text or display advertisement online on a search engine or Web page.
infographic	Taking a concept or statistics and creating a visually appealing graphic for it. This is a popular way to create content which attracts people to link to it from their Web sites.
internet yellow pages	Internet Yellow Pages - the Internet version of the traditional yellow pages. Examples include Superpages.com, CitySearch.com and InsiderPages.com. These can be helpful for getting your sites found locally.
IYP	see internet yellow pages
Javascript	A Web technology used in some Web sites which, when activated, causes an action to occur. Javascript can be used in menus where clicking or hovering over a menu can cause it to expand with more menu options. Javascript menus can cause some trouble for search engines in terms of activating them and following the links contained within. It's recommended to include HTML menus in addition to Javascript menus.
keyphrase	Keyphrase is the same as Keyword Phrase. See keyword phrase.
keyword	Keywords are the words that a company or person wants their Web site to be found for. Often used interchangeably with keyword phrase or keyphrase because most searches are of more than one keyword.
keyword phrase	Phrases that people use in search engines to find what they're looking for. It can include any number of words (1+) or even just acronyms (type "seo" into your search engine to see what I mean). Your business can target keyword phrases to improve your "findability" in the search engines.
keyword stuffing	Excessive use of keywords in any part of a Web site including the Page Title, Description Meta Tag, Keyword Meta Tag, Picture Alt Tags or the content. Avoid this as it makes your site look spammy to users and possibly to search engines!
landing page	A page designed for visitors that is aligned with an advertising message, specific target keywords and specific conversion goals.
link	See hyperlink
link juice	A search engine agnostic way of describing the search engine value passed by links from one Web site to another
link-building	The activities done to ask for, buy or attract inbound links to ones Web pages.

local	Used to describe local businesses that need local customers (as opposed to national or international customers) or search engines that are serving up local search results
meta description tag	A tag on a Web page that allows the Web site owner to describe the page. Search engines will often (but not always) use the information in the Meta Description tag as the 2nd and 3rd lines of a search engine result for that page.
meta keywords tag	A meta tag that is placed in the code of a Web page that allows the Web site owner to place keyword phrases (separated by commas) that he/she wants to be found for by search engines. This tag is generally considered to have no value by the search engines (but some people still use it for keywords, misspellings or synonyms of target phrases)
meta tag	Meta tags are HTML code that allow Web site owners to communicate with the search engine spiders about very specific areas. For example, meta description tags, canonical tags and meta keywords tags are meta tags.
micro-blogging	The act of writing short posts using a platform designed for these shorter posts via sites such as Twitter or Yammer. Twitter is the most common micro-blogging platform.
Microsoft Adcenter	Microsoft's pay per click system which competes with Google Adwords.
natural search results	see organic search results
no follow tag	A tag that can be applied to links on a Web site creating a "nofollow link". Use of no follow links means the Web site owner does not want the search engines to count these links for passing of Google PageRank or "link juice" to the page being linked to.
off-page SEO	The activities performed outside of a Web site to improve the rank of a site's pages in the search engines. The main off-page SEO activities are link-building activities designed to increase the number of inbound links back to a Web site.
on-page SEO	The activities performed on a Web site to improve the rank of a site's pages in the search engines. These can involve using keywords in strategic places such as page titles, headers, within the content, in file names, internal links and more.
Open Directory Project (www.DMOZ.org)	A directory of Web sites that is managed by volunteers. Web sites are organized by categories. Getting a listing in the Open Directory Project is usually considered to be valuable for SEO and you can request that your site be listed. It's typically very hard to get listed due to the volume of requests, the limitations of the curators, and the requirement for the site to offer unique content. Google sometimes uses the descriptions on www.DMOZ.org as part of the search result for sites that have listings.

organic search results　　Non-paid search results that display links to pages, documents, videos or other content that the search engine deems decides are the most relevant for a given search. Also called Natural Search Results

page title　　Code that allows Web site owners to put a page title for each Web page in their site. Generally considered the most important "on page SEO" tactic to help with ranking a site.

paid listings　　Paying to have your Web site listed (with a link) on a site or directory

Paid Search Results　　Can include text ads, banner ads, product ads or other. They will usually say "sponsored results" and will usually be separate from non-paid (or organic results).

plugins　　Plugins are add-ons to a software platform such as the Firefox Web browser or Wordpress. These plug-ins provide enhanced functionality for the tool being added to. Often these are free but there are also for fee plugins.

PPC – "Pay Per Click"　　Google and Bing and some other search engines have pay per click advertising systems (which puts your ad in the Paid Search Results described above).

rank　　The order that pages come up in a search engine is called rank. To get a site to rank well is to have it come up high in the search engine results pages (SERPs) for a particular keyword.

real-time　　Something occurring as another event occurs. For example, real time search is the ability to search on topics that are occurring now or very recently. The search engines are increasingly including real-time search results in searches that warrant up-to-date information.

relevancy　　How closely a search result matches (or is relevant for) the keywords used in a given search query.

RSS feed　　A technology that allows someone to subscribe to your blog posts and read them on an RSS reader or via email. When you publish a blog post the RSS feed for that post is generated and sent to your subscribers.

search algorithm　　The mathematical formulas that rank the search results pages when a search query is typed into a search engine. These are closely guarded secrets by the search engines because they don't want people to be able to game the system and focus excessive attention on the factors that cause sites to rank.

search box　　The box on a Web browser or on a Web page where a searcher types in a search query (made up of keywords).

search engine spiders	Automated bots from the search engines that crawl the Internet to index pages, follow links and discover new sites and pages.
search query	A specific search in a search engine. The query is the search phrase your are using to perform the search.
SEM (Search Engine Marketing)	Search Engine Marketing (or SEM) usually implies the activities involved with pay per click advertising on Web sites (as opposed to SEO which implies getting on the search engines without paying them.
SEO (Search Engine Optimization)	SEO means the activities performed to get a page to rank in the organic (or natural) search results in the search engines.
SERP	Search Engine Results Page. The page that comes up when you type in a search term or phrase into a search engine such as Google, Yahoo or Bing. It's filled with links to Web pages and possibly maps, videos, pictures and more.
shareability	How attractive a piece of content is for sharing and how easily it can be shared (e.g. via share buttons)
sitemap	A map of a site's key pages with links to those pages. Usually designed for people or for search engines to crawl the site. This is different from an XML site map which is designed only for search engines.
snippet	The portion of an individual search result, under the title of the Web page, which describes the Web page. This snippet is created by a search engine. In Google's case, the snippet comes from a choice or combination of 1) Meta Description Tag – a tag that you can fill in for each page of your Web site. It's embedded in your Web site code 2) Content from your Web site – Google may automatically extract some text from your Web site to use in the snippet 3) Open Directory Project description. If your site is listed in the Open Directory Project, Google may use part of the description on that site for your snippet (www.DMOZ.org).
Social Bookmarking	Sites that allow users to add new URLs for others to view. They also include the ability for users to rate the content and for people to connect with others to form networks.
Social Media	Social Media is a term used for online Web sites, tools or applications that involve social activities or communication amongst the participants as a key part of its model. For example, YouTube.com allows for users to contribute, share, rank, respond to and repost (on their own Web sites) video clips. Facebook allows users to post to their own "wall", to post on other people's walls, to directly communicate with other users, to share various media (pictures, videos), to follow the Facebook pages of groups he/she likes or to play socially-focused games together. Other examples of Social Media sites include LinkedIn (more business focused), Twitter (short posts or "micro-blogging"), MySpace, Plaxo and even a Blog (which allows for interaction between blogger and audience.

Social Networking Similar to Social Media, a term to describe sites primarily focused on networking online. For example LinkedIn and Plaxo are more business-focused "Social Networking sites". Facebook, Twitter and MySpace are a mix of non-business and business for social networking. Social Media and Social Networking are sometimes used interchangeably.

Spam Usage of a Web-based tool that results in unwanted content. Can include spam emails which result in clogged inboxes, spam comments on blogs that are advertising products, services or Web sites such as Viagra or pornography sites, comments in Web-based forums that don't provide help but merely push their agenda, user review sites filled with text and links and more.

spam or spammy Excessive unwanted advertising in email, on Web sites, in blog comments or in forums.

stemming Expanding keywords by adding suffixes, tense or "s". For example run, runs, running, runner. In Google Adwords and Bing (Microsoft Adcenter) the advertiser needs to account for these variations.

textual content Content on a Web site that is mainly made up of text. If done in standard HTML, this content is easily crawled and read by search engines.

time on site The amount of time a visitor spends on a site. Web site analytics can measure this.

TLD Top level domain. The highest level of the Web site address such as ".com", ".net", ".org", ".tv" and many others. These TLDs are limited and often lead to scarcity in the most popular ones such as short, meaningful names with the .com TLD.

toolbar A bar on a Web browser such as Internet Explorer or Firefox that includes various tools. There are a variety of SEO toolbars that can be added using Firefox or Chrome plugins. Also, the Google Toolbar is available on Internet Explorer and includes a search box (directly to Google) as well as the Toolbar PageRank of the current site and other Google-related tools.

top level domain see TLD

top pages In Web site analytics the top pages report shows the top pages visited and the time spend on these pages.

traffic sources In Web site analytics the traffic sources report shows where traffic is coming from. For example which search engines, which Web sites or whether the visitor came from directly typing in the URL (see URL).

trust A factor that helps sites rank higher in the search engines. Based on different factors, including what sites are linking to your pages, a Web site can build up more trust in the eyes of the search engines.

unique visitors A new visitor to a Web site. Web site analytics programs can track the number of unique visitors coming to your site in a given time period (such as day, month or year)

universal search   When search engines include a variety of information in a SERP (search engine results page) such as a map, stock quote, link to videos, pictures, content from Social Media sites in addition to links or documents (which were in traditional search results).

URL   Universal Resource Locator or, colloquially, your Web page's address. For example. http://www.example.com and http://www.example.com/services are the URLs for two pages on the Example.com Web site.

video ad   An advertisement in the form of a video.

viral   Something is said to have "gone viral" when a particular piece of content (article, video, top 10 list, picture) spreads quickly via Social Media platforms such as YouTube, Facebook, Twitter or via email.

Web browser   An Internet tool designed to display Web pages. Top Web browsers on computers include Internet Explorer, Firefox, Safari and Chrome. On phones, browsers include Internet Explorer, Safari, Opera and more.

weblog   The original term for a blog (see blog above)

White Hat SEO   People who perform SEO that is considered legitimate by the Search Engines. This can include using the appropriate tags in Web sites, putting in useful content that is helpful for people and that helps search engines understand the purpose of the Web site and creating great content that leads other Web sites to link to your site.

XML sitemap   A sitemap of the main pages of a Web site created in the XML Web language which can easily be read by search engines. An XML sitemap can be created and submitted to the search engines to help them index the site correctly.

Yahoo   Previously the #2 search engine in the US. Yahoo also has a lot of its own original content, separate from the content linked to from the search engine. In August of 2010 it combined forces with Bing and started to use Bing's search results in place of Yahoo's own results.